HOLY SH*T

I'M A FU***NG PSYCHIC

REAL LIFE STORIES OF HOW
I BECAME A PSYCHIC HEALER

By: Veronica Belakova

STOP HERE IF YOU ARE OFFENDED BY THE TITLE OF THIS BOOK

DISCLAIMER:

1.   Like in all my books, I guarantee that you will find a bunch of typos and grammatical errors because I self-edit and self-publish my books.

An actual quote from a book critic on "Good Reads" about my first book:

"Completely unedited, containing typos, which, admittedly, as a linguist and a perfectionist, I initially found disturbing, only to realise it makes the experience even more real as the author is not an English native speaker and does not really care about technicalities."

*She misspelled "realize"

2.   This book is riddled with a shit ton of swear words.

Like most humans that believe in a higher power like God, we mostly pray with our mind or with our thoughts. (Unless you are a religious fanatic that screams prayers in church so others can hear how holy you are) My thoughts do not change when I speak to MY God. In fact, they run wild because nobody else can hear them. I have always cursed when praying or talking shit to MY God and he has never cared or condemned me. In fact, we've shared some good laughs. So, I figured since this is the way I have always prayed and talked to MY God, why fake it for this book?

3.   This book is meant to entertain you with my TRUE-LIFE events.

If you are a skeptic, I invite you to read this book and get mind fucked just like I do every day.

4.   ALL OF THE STORIES IN THIS BOOK ARE REAL AND TRUE. ALL OF THE PEOPLE CAN BE INTERVIEWED ABOUT THEIR PSYCHIC SESSION. NO NAMES HAVE BEEN CHANGED BECAUSE THEN I WOULD HAVE TO NAME THEM ALL BURGER.

This book is dedicated to: The person in whose presence I fell in love with myself. My number one cheerleader and kindest critic. The only woman and the best man I have ever been with. The one I will love for eternity. And lest we forget, the only woman in the world whose tattoo art is certified as contemporary fine art by the MACRO museum in Rome and the best tattoo artist that every lived, Ivana Tattoo Art.

Introduction

Hello, my name is Veronica. I call myself the psychic healer. You know, it is still very weird for me to say that I am a psychic healer because like many of you, I was a hard-core skeptic. I did not believe in anything that had to do with psychics, palm readers, fortune tellers, etc. Anytime anybody brought up something about that world I pushed it off as hippie and woo woo. I even thought of it as tree hugger shit or even considered it to be witchcraft. But mostly, I always smiled and thought "to each its own."

I was born in ciudad Juarez Mexico. I was raised in extreme poverty by my sweet grandmother, a very spiritual woman that made me believe that I was the funniest human on the planet. As a small child and without the knowledge of religion, I nurtured a relationship with my God, my higher power. Before I could pronounce my "R's" I established a tight connection with God. I made childhood demands in my prayers and refused No as any of God's answers.

At the age of 6 years old, I was kidnapped by my mother and smuggled into America into a life of sexual abuse and horror. At fifteen, I ran away from home and was forced to drop out of school.

My first book "My Life My Story, God, You Owe Me" shares more details of my fucked-up life. Despite all the horrible things I put up with, I never strayed far from my relationship with God. In fact, I demanded more answers. Because, why the fuck not?

For most of my twenties and thirties, I felt like I was swimming in an ocean filled with sharks. No matter how hard I tried to survive I felt like my hands were tied down behind my back, my eyes pulled out from my sockets, and someone upstairs was having a good laugh. Yet, somehow, I managed to survive. (As a highly functioning addict, but hey I survived)

After a divorce that kicked my ass, I found myself alone, homeless, penniless, living in my car and addicted to crystal meth. I felt like I escaped the sharks, but I had sunk in the ocean and hit rock bottom!

One day, I found myself in a hotel room in a paranoid schizophrenic daze. I knew that the only way to save myself was to swim up. I crawled out of the bathtub where I had been hiding for several days and carefully turned on the light. For the first time in a long time, I saw myself. I took a deep breath and almost collapsed as a scared human stared back in the mirror.

In my reflection, I saw a pile of skin and bones at a merely eighty-eight pounds and I was moved. And, that day, I made a deal with God. I decided that from that moment on I would take better care of myself. I threw my life, the bag of crystal meth, in the toilet and with tears flowing down my face I flushed it down with the hope of a new life. That moment, I felt from the depths of my anxiety a strange calmness arise. A seance of peace. I talk about that experience as the central defining experience of my life. That is when a fundamental change occurred, which I deemed necessary to free myself from my profound ancestral rooted addiction that had not only defined but also consumed me. If I am alive, it is because of that moment.

I began to slowly rebuild my life. I quit drugs cold turkey, no rehab. About ten years have passed since I made that wise choice. In the process of self-healing, I created a life as a broken human. I surrounded myself with people that never cared about me in a life built for social media. I had everything a girl could ever want but, in the process, I never healed from my traumas. I built a profitable business and was drug free but drinking Belvedere dirty martinis every day. One day, I had an aha moment and I decided to quit that life cold turkey. I left everything behind (except my business) and decided to live my life in my own journey and jump into my own fucking lane. I sobered up and focused on living a clean life.

I felt like I was finally living my true authentic self. I met a woman whom I decided to date. We traveled the world together, erasing stigmas, removing boundaries, and breaking down barriers. I fell in love with myself more and more every day.

One day in October of 2021, while traveling the Galapagos Islands, my life was turned upside down. I experienced a miracle working in me and through me. An interaction with my server, someone whom I didn't know anything about awakened my psychic abilities.

Within the next couple of days, I was off the coast of Africa in the Canary Islands. Out of nowhere I was overtaken by powerful psychic abilities that exuded out of me so naturally that I could not deny their existence. I began seeing signs and giving psychic readings to many strangers whose lives were changed for the better.

When I arrived in Slovakia a week later, I had time to process what was going on and a whole world of questions began to pour in, and doubts took over me. I asked myself,

"Is this from God?"

"Is this from the devil?"

"What is going on with me?"

One day in the shower, where I do most of my thinking, I heard a voice that said, "Be at peace, every human is born with this gift but most of you are afraid to use it."

After this message, I began to let go. I began to make friends with my new gift and with ease my psychic abilities took over. They began to grow stronger and stronger, and I began to read everyone that needed to hear a word of encouragement, heed to medical direction, those who simply needed to feel the holy presence of God, and a couple of people whose past loved ones had a message of hope to share with them through me.

After weeks of never-ending psychic readings, my psychic and healing abilities blew my mind and the minds of those around me.

I truly believe that if this would not have happened to me, I would still be a skeptic. I would also have more time on my hands to continue writing my other books. But I chose to write

9

this booklet in-between because I still can't believe I'M A FUCKING PSYCHIC!

HOW IT STARTED...

GALAPAGOS / OCT. 2021

CASE NAME: **BE WITH ANGELICA**

Picture this, Ivana and I were on a delightful trip aboard Celebrity Cruises Mega Yach Flora in the Galapagos Islands celebrating her birthday. We were the first passengers allowed back after Covid and shared the ship with about forty other people.

Our day started out with magic from the moment we woke up. We sipped our coffee and watched whales swim in the distance. It was fucking surreal. While getting ready for our excursion, we heard commotion and me being little Ms. Nosey and Ivana being super curious, we ran out in our robes to see what the chatter was. Our minds were blown when we saw a whale giving birth to her baby just a few yards away from our ship.

Holy   shit,   right?

After this miraculous site, I dressed up like Indiana Jones (for Instagram pics) and we all jumped on a tinder to go hike up a volcano. It was like fucking national geographic threw up all over the place. I heard that Galapagos was insane, but fuck I wasn't ready for all the weird shit I saw. I instantly identified with the ugliest iguanas that laid all over the place spitting and mad dogging each other. I gawked at our resemblance.

While the others ventured off and as Ivana took five thousand pictures of the same damn cactus, I wondered off and found a

11

beautiful pond of trapped rainwater in one of the volcanos craters.

As I hiked the volcano, I noticed a guide close by. "Would it be possible for me to hike down there and touch the water?" I asked hoping he would understand.

"Oh, No Mam, we cannot go there, that is forbidden, he said in his broken English.

"¿Puedo ir para aya a tocar el agua?," I asked in Spanish just in case it would work.

"No," he answered. I don't know if it was in English or Spanish but, I knew it was a no go.

I walked as close as I could to the water and for some reason, I found myself doing some holy santo prayer towards the water.

As I walked away, he stopped me and motioned me to go ahead.

"Go mam, you can go to the water," he said smiling.

I walked slowly down the crater and reached into the warm water. I began splashing it all over me in a cross like motion.

Suddenly Walter Mercado, I mean Ivana was next to me splashing herself too. We laughed and continued our adventure.

We returned to the ship later that evening and got dolled up for din din. Because of the low number of passengers on the ship, the restaurant was virtually empty. We sat alone at a table for twelve. We giggled with pleasure as we zipped champagned and ordered our dinner. As we talked about our adventures on the island of Santa Cruz, my server placed my meal in front of me. And, as his hand passed my face, I touched the side of it and said,

"You need to be with Angelica."

And I turned my chair so that I could see his face. I was stunned at the words coming out of my mouth. I looked into his eyes, and he was sincerely shocked. Seeing his expression scared me. Suddenly, I said again,

"You need to be with Angelica."

"What did you say?" he asked.

I quickly replied, "be with Angelica." I felt like my mouth was moving without my permission.

"You know her?" he asked.

"No, I don't," I answered.

"Then why do you say these things to me?"

"Is she your room attendant?"

"Did she tell you about us?"

I looked at him ignoring his questions.

"Listen I don't know her; I don't know you." "I do know that you two should be together!"

He turned pale and walked away as fast as he could.

I turned back to Ivana and asked, "Am I drunk?"

I was hoping she would say yes, so that we would continue to wine and dine.

"No babe, you're fine," she said.

Then she asked, "is something wrong?"

"When our server comes back here, ask him what I told him," I said quickly.

HOLY SH*T I'M A F***NG PSYCHIC

The server approached our table but avoided my side, he poured Ivana more champagne.

"Excuse me, what Veronica tell you?"

She asked him in her heavy accent.

He quickly asked, "do you know her?"

"Is she your room attendant?"

"Why does she say these things to me?"

"What did she say?" Ivana asked.

"She told me that I should be with Angelica!"

"Did she tell you ladies about us?"

"We want to be together it has just been hard for us"

"We are scheduled to see each other tomorrow when I get off the ship."

"I was thinking about not going because it's complicated with work but after this, I am definitely going to be with her."

"Thank you so much," he said.

He went on to tell me their story which, honestly, I really don't remember.

He walked away shaken but happy. Ivana looked at me and asked, "how the fuck did you know that?"

"I don't know," I said.

"I felt like my mouth was moving by itself."

It was so strange that we both decided to ignore the whole thing and instead of trying to understand it we ordered another bottle of champagne.

SLOVAKIA / OCT. 2021

CASE NAME: SOMETHING'S UP

We jumped on a plane and headed to Slovakia. As soon as we landed, we were rushed to a podcast. Ivana was filming a segment with one of Slovakia's A list celebrities. I watched them talk back and forth. I cozied up in a spot where no one could really see me with the intention of falling asleep. I woke myself up as the back of my head hit the wall and my mouth ached from being forced open as I slept.

I gathered myself and wiped my slobber with my vintage Chanel sleeve when suddenly I saw a rash forming on the host's neck. I thought I was dreaming.

"Holy shit!" I thought! I wiped my eyes carefully making sure not to rub off my mascara and looked again at his neck.

His freaking neck was on fire! It was burning around his golden necklace. I blinked my eyes like a crazy woman as many times as I could, but the rash looked even worse.

I wanted to stand up and walk towards them, but I calmed myself down and told myself I was jet lagged.

As soon as we jumped in the car, I insisted that Ivana call the guy and tell him to stop wearing that necklace. Perhaps he was allergic to it.

"Why would I do that?" she asked.

"Just do it!" I said forcefully.

"Are you fucked up?" she added.

15

HOLY SH*T I'M A F***NG PSYCHIC

"No!" I said. "He has a bad rash on the back of his neck, I could see it. She looked at me and said, "he does not have a rash, I was close to him!"
"I am not going to call him and sound crazy!"
"Do it!" I said.
"What the fuck am I supposed to say?" she asked as she texted him carefully.
"Tell him perhaps to take a break from that necklace."
Ivana did and he had many questions. To which I had no answers to.........yet

MYJAVA, SLOVAKIA / NOV. 2021

CASE NAME: I CAN SMELL YOUR BLOOD

That same night, we arrived in Myjava, one of my favorite little towns in the world. I think the first time in my life when I felt safe from the financial mind fuck in my head was in this tiny little town. Myjava is also dear to my heart because it is home to the first group of friends I ever made in Slovakia and the first place where the first draft of my first book was printed. "My Life My Story, God, You Owe Me, a cluster fuck of memories of the shitty life I lived before God stopped owing me. Yeah, it took some huge ass balls to write that book so buy it, read it, and give me a good review on Amazon.

So, get ready for this one!

If you are lucky enough to be Slovakian, you know about wellness.

HOLY SH*T I'M A F***NG PSYCHIC

In Slovakia they have wellness time, yes you read that right....
Wellness time! Employers allocate time for their employees to
take fully paid days off work for wellness. Super cool, I think.

Everyone is all about it, so of course after dinner at our favorite
restaurant, I joined the gals at the spa for wellness time.

Ivana on the other hand, joined the guys at the only bar on the
street with the intention of drinking every bottle of champagne
the tiny town had stocked up for that year.

I struggled to breathe in the steam room and my chubby
stomach muscle ached from being sucked in order to keep up
with the glorious Slovakian bodies that surrounded me. So, I
quickly made my exit and slid into my Bottega boots. I
wondered alone down the snowy street to join the others at the
bar.

I entered the packed bar and found the only empty stool at the
bar. It so happened to be next to the only human that
somewhat spoke English in the entire bar. Besides my friends of
course, but they were on the third bottle of champagne and had
no interest in pretending they understood what I was saying.

I looked over at the fellow that sat next to me and said,

"Don't travel anywhere yet, I am so sorry, but your mom will
die of cancer."

I instantly cringed at the words coming out of my mouth. I
quickly reached for my covid mask hoping it would shut me the
fuck up. But I didn't have one.

He looked mind fucked and asked,

"What did you just say?"

HOLY SH*T I'M A F***NG PSYCHIC

"I am so sorry, but your mom will die of cancer," I replied again cringing at my voice. Then as if I did not just step in shit, I added, "She will die soon so don't you dare go anywhere."

His tears began to flow as he said, "Yes, she is dying, and I am very sad."

I stared at him.

What the fuck did he just say? I looked around hoping I was dreaming. Maybe I had passed out in the sauna and the girls left me behind unable to carry my chubby little body out.

"I was planning to travel," he added.

"No!" I exclaimed.

"You cannot go, she will die when you do, and you will feel guilty for leaving."

Before he could sucker punch me, I asked him to give me his arm.

He wiped his tears and obeyed.

I lifted his sleeve and began drawing with my finger a tree of life on his arm and giving him instructions from his ancestors imbedded in his DNA.

At this point I figure, fuck just keep digging your grave why stop now!

So, I continued.

"Do not be afraid when she goes."

"She will always give you signs, I promise"

HOLY SH*T I'M A F***NG PSYCHIC

Suddenly, he feverishly lifted his other sleeve and showed me the tree of life I had just drawn on his arm was tattooed on his other arm.

We both pushed each other away and he yelled for Ivana.

Ivana ran to us, as I screamed out,

"I can smell your blood!"

"It's a different type of blood," I said.

Ivana looked at me in shock. (Well one of her eyes looked at me and the other looked the other way, her eyes tend to cross after the fourth glass of champagne.)

"Why would you tell him that?" she yelled.

"Don't say those things," she added.

"Tell him I can smell his blood!" I said.

"Yes!"

"Yes!" he said more mind fucked than before.

"I have O negative blood!"

By this time, he was sobbing and suddenly he forgot how to speak English. As for me, I was done. The message was over, and the smell was gone.

"Let's go home," I said to Ivana.

We got into our taxi and Ivana said,

"You were drunk, don't worry, you were drunk!"

I knew that I was not drunk but happily agreed, so I didn't say a word. (That is rare for me.)

The next day we woke up and looked at each other.

"What the holy fuck was that?" she asked.

"Even if you were drunk, that shit was weird!" she said.

HOLY SH*T I'M A F***NG PSYCHIC

"How did you do that?"
"How did you know?"
"I have no idea, I said.
We left it alone and jumped on a plane headed towards Tenerife.

TENERIFE ISLAND / NOV. 2021

CASE NAME: AMOR PROPIO

As a frenzy of photographers and Instagramers flocked around Ivana, I checked my reflection in the mirror to ensure my gut remained hidden from the sea of endless photographs. In the reflection, I could see Ivana in her glory as more and more celebrities gathered around her all aiming to be the next lucky one to boast clever hashtags of their time with the tattoo queen.

I watched from close by as her smile lit up their Faceapps when suddenly a beautiful woman hugged on to her and posed for the camera. Normally I would have cut a bitch, but this time I approached her and stopped the flashes so that I could fix her Spanx. (If you know you know.)

When I touched her, I heard a voice instruct me to tell her,
"You need to stop giving away all of your love!"
"You give away all of you, everything, every day to everyone and get nothing in return."

HOLY SH*T I'M A F***NG PSYCHIC

"When are you going to stop?"

I began speaking the words aloud just as quickly as they came to my mind, almost in a form of translation.

When they finished with their pictures, she quickly approached me and looked directly into my eyes and asked,

"How do you know all about me?"

"Who told you about me?"

I was mind fucked!

Ivana approached us I think because she thought that I was about to take off my earrings and bitch slap that lady ghetto style. Because of the tone in my voice.

The woman asked Ivana to translate. She began to spill the beans about her life and how she was fed up and running on empty. Of course, I did not understand because she spoke in Slovakian language.

I then said,

"Self-love," as I touched her shoulder.

"Focus now on Self-love."

"Today is the day you get stopped by love and given a sign from the stars!"

She was in shock and pulled her dress off the shoulder I had just touched and revealed a star tattoo.

I   about   shit   myself!

What in the world just happened again?

I had never seen this woman! I hurried off as another group gathered hoping to snap an Instagram pic that would make them instafamous. I made my way to my seat when suddenly,

HOLY SH*T I'M A F***NG PSYCHIC

CASE NAME: FALL IN LOVE WITH THE MIC

A woman tapped me on my shoulder.

"Excuse me," she said.

I turned around to notice she was intending to sit, and my chair was in her way. She was stunning, of glorious stature, picturesque, a celebrity straight from the movies. Instead of expressing my awe of her, my mouth blurted out,

"Immediately take that choker off your neck!"

She looked stunned and responded in shock.

"Excuse me!"

I turned my chair to face her.

She smiled but looked at me like she was about to slap me.

"What did you just say?"

"Take that choker off your neck!" I commanded again.

She held on to her seat and slid down grabbing on firmly to her glittery choker as if she were melting into the ground.

Again, I commanded, "take that choker off your neck!"

I watched as her eyes grw and her hands grabbed on to the back of her neck quickly loosening the clutch from her choker.

"You have a blockage on your voice!"

"It's time for you to release it!"

"It's time for you to use your voice and sing out loud!"

"Grab ahold of that mic and love it!"

"Fall in love with the mic again!"

"Sing to the world!"

"Sing out loud!"

HOLY SH*T I'M A F***NG PSYCHIC

Her eyes popped out and her jaw dropped. Suddenly Ivana ran over to see what all the commotion was.

"Sit here and translate for me," I said as I pointed at a chair next to me.

I began telling the woman that she had several blockages, and they were holding her back. I told her how they were all located on her left side of her body and touched her left eye. She began to smile and nod.

"Yes, yes, a shaman from Mexico told me the same thing," she said.

Ivana's eyes bulged out of her head. I then grabbed ahold of the woman and said,

"Go and use your voice and sing to the masses sing to the masses!"

She hugged me and thanked me. I turned my chair around like if nothing had happened. I could not wrap my mind around what was happening. Ivana sat next to me. We looked at each other and she said, "babe, I think you're psychic!"

Next thing I know, the lady is on stage and singing to the crowd. I turned to look at everyone at my table and quickly began "reading" everyone else sitting with us at our table.

Long story short this beautiful lady was the invited performer who was supposed to sing to the guests at the party. Unfortunately, that morning she suffered an anxiety attack and cancelled her performance. But after my psychic reading, she grabbed the mic and sang for the first time in nine years. After that she released her single which went viral on YouTube.

CASE NAME: WORSHIP HER FEET

The next day I woke up exhausted and noticed a huge bruise on my ribs. I am naturally lethargic unless I am shopping or eating but this exhaustion was debilitating. I could not move all day. I laid around catching rays on a lawn chair wondering what the hell happened last night. I freaked out more and more with each memory.

After a while Ivana finally got the nerve to ask me,

"Babe, what the hell is going on?"

"Are you a freaking psychic?"

"I am speechless," I said hoping the past events were made up stories in my head.

"Do you want to see something weird?" I asked.

"More weird than last night?" she replied.

I lifted my shirt and showed her my bruise.

"What the hell!"

"How did you get that?"

"Did you fall?"

"No, I didn't fall you were with me all night!"

"I don't know what's going on, I am completely lost."

I gathered enough energy to slide into something that required no effort. I smothered myself with a ridiculous amount of sunscreen, threw on large sunglasses, and jumped into our rental car. We drove down the islands majestic coastline to meet some influencers at a villa they had rented. The energy of the island was so strong. I rolled down the window and smelled

HOLY SH*T I'M A F***NG PSYCHIC

the volcanic air and instantly I floated into an overwhelming state of gratitude.

When we arrived, it was nothing like I had imagined. The influencers were kind normal people. I don't know why I assumed they would be commercial statues with no emotion or attachment to real conversations. No one was on their phones like I assumed instead, they all made coffee and treats to welcome us in.

The villa was all I imagined. Glorious.

As I took all of this in, I felt a whispering energy deep within me.

Everyone that was there was also at the party the night before and word got out faster than Will smith got up to slap Chris Rock. Needless to say, everyone had questions and wanted a psychic reading.

Ivana told them that I was very tired and was not prepared.

However, a thin woman approached us as we made our way outside and begged for me to intervene.

I looked deep into her beautiful eyes; they reminded me of Egypt. (I haven't been there, yet)

Without hesitation, I told her to raise her arm over her head. I motioned for her to mimic my movements as I lifted my arm. The movement made the bruised area on my body ache.

"I can't do that," she said softly.

I knew instantly that the bruise on my ribs was hers. I knew her pain.

HOLY SH*T I'M A F***NG PSYCHIC

I got behind her, closed my eyes tight, and began rubbing her neck and sweeping the energy in a downward motion off her body.

Then suddenly, I dropped to the floor. When I say dropped, I mean drop stomach to floor, face plant, and tits flat up against the cold ground.

I laid on the floor with my eyes closed then I got onto my knees and began rubbing the back of her ankles. I then heard a voice within me say,

"Worship her feet."

Still, with my eyes closed, I grabbed one of her ankles and began hugging on to them. In my head I thanked her. I felt a deep love flow through me. I was so moved that I couldn't let go. I don't know how much time passed. I held on to her ankles and loved on her, I was so grateful for our lives in Egypt. As my hand got closer to her toes the urge to kiss her foot took over me.

That's when I freaked out and I opened my eyes and saw that her toes were webbed. I placed her foot down and looked at her other foot. It too was webbed.

I was then able to tell her that she had a parasite from her past life.

"Should I go get surgery," she asked me holding back her tears.

"Yes, you should go quickly," I said calmly.

"But I'm scared, the doctor said that it's a fifty - fifty chance that I die on the surgical bed!"

I told her, "You will not die, and you know this."

"Take a deep breath and feel your answer deep inside you!"

HOLY SH*T I'M A F***NG PSYCHIC

"You will not die!"
I cupped my hands and placed them in front of her and said,
"GIVE IT TO ME NOW!"
"What?" she asked terrified.
I moved my cupped hands even closer this time and again said,
"GIVE IT TO ME NOW!"
"Why?" she asked.
"Are you sure?"
"Aren't you scared?"
Time stood still and I felt the hot island sun on my back and the moist grass on my feet. I felt the love of God all around me.
NO, I nodded while smiling. I got closer to her face and looked deep into her majestic Egyptian eyes. She stared into mine with fear as her eyelashes stood still. I filled her corneas with peace, then moved into her pupils. Our eyes didn't blink, I followed her eyes down into her heart, then into her stomach. Within seconds, I had wrapped my love around her and filled her with peace.
"I take all illness from you and proclaim you healed."
She smiled in disbelief.
"From now on know that no matter what anyone tells you about your health, you and only you have the answers within you. They are in your stomach. This parasite comes from your past life, but you will be fine.
"Go home and get the surgery, remove the parasite."
"Don't be scared anymore because it will not kill you."
She thanked me and we hugged.

27

HOLY SH*T I'M A F***NG PSYCHIC

In the car on the way back to our hotel, a bit of fear took over me. What the hell did I just do? I wondered if the parasite was now inside me. What if I just got a parasite that would kill me?

I heard the voice of God say, "just do your breath work, you will be fine, stop being a little bitch."

I rolled down the window and began a series of weird ass breathing exercises. I blew out my breath out into the island's hot air. Somehow, I knew these breaths were necessary to breathe out the illness I had just taken from her body.

I took a quick look at Ivana. She looked confused but that's not unusual, especially when I'm doing one of my singing or gum Instagram stories.

"What now?" Ivana asked.

"What the heck are you doing now?"

I was beginning to get a bit dizzy, so I sat back and relaxed.

"I'm breathing her illness out of my body," I answered calmly.

"What illness," she asked.

"The one I took from her body," I replied calmly.

"Are you afraid?" she asked.

"Not anymore," I answered then I passed out.

*Later that year, I found out that she did have surgery, and she did survive, and she is doing well awaiting an organ transfer.

CASE STUDY: WE ARE ALL BORN WITH THIS GIFT

When we returned to the hotel, I knew something was up. I mean why was I acting like a modern version of a holy santo? The behavior I was exuding was simply not me.

We continued to ignore what had been happening and I could sense that Ivana was taken back.

That night in the shower I prayed to God.

"God is this from the devil?" I asked scrubbing myself.

"What the fuck is going on?"

"I don't ever want to sin against you but this shit's getting weird.

"I feel like it is taking a hold of me, and I have no control over it."

As I waited for an answer, yes, I wait for answers when I pray. Some people call that meditation.

I realized how I have always been extremely empathetic. I have always felt such a deep connection to the suffering of others. Someone once told me that I was addicted to the suffering of other souls. They went as far as instructing me to look away when I felt the pain of the homeless on the street or the pain of the beggars that always approached me on my travels. That person recommended that I look away from the sick and the innocent. It simply is not your journey, that person said. But I just could never help myself. My heart has always ached from the pain of others.

As I had this realization, I heard the voice of God.

"You are all born with this gift, Veronica."

"Every human is born with this gift but so many are afraid to use it!"

"You are all equipped with the gift of healing each other, find it as a blessing, use it to help others."

"Do not be afraid."

"In moments of doubt, stand fast in your faith."

As water washed over me, I closed my eyes and visualized myself in front of a large crowd. Healing and performing miracle healings.

I thanked the holy water as I turned it off. Then, I prayed.

"Ok, God, if this shit is real, I want to heal the disabled and the ones in wheelchairs."

"If I am going to let go and look like and act like a fool, I want real fucking miracles. I am not settling for mediocre shit.

CASE STUDY: I CAN "READ" EVERYONE

After that, I began to read everyone. I knew almost everything about that person. I could see it in their skin, their hands, their clothes, their eyes, their teeth, their moles, in their wrinkles, and in anything that I looked at. I saw answers on their ears, heard messages in the song that was playing. Answers started flowing like a miracle and everything I would say to them was always a message of love, hope, and kindness.

I quickly, began to experience extreme sensitivity to energy. I didn't know yet, but I would begin to suffer the ailments of people I would come in contact within my near future.

CASE STUDY: I FEEL NAUSEOUS

As we wrapped up our time on Tenerife Island, I began to embody the miracle of God's new gift working through me. As we got ready to visit our friend's home to say goodbye, I began to feel nauseous.

When I arrived at their home, instead of being attracted to the champagne or the impressive view, I was attracted to her youngest son. I just wanted to give him so much love. I loved him dearly, like a child. I don't have any children, nor did I ever want them, but I felt a motherly love. So strong.

I said to my friend, "please love him and watch him closely."

"Watch him carefully, he needs so much close love and attention right now."

Listen, I love kids and all, but I'm not all about them. I would rather talk about business or travel, not kids.

But the love and attraction I instantly felt for this kid was undeniable. Almost like the love I have for a first-class airplane ticket.

My friend said, "Oh my God, Veronica thank you so much for saying that he was actually very nauseous all night."

If it had been another time, I would have thought. "Oh my gosh that's such a coincidence!"

By now, I knew that nothing is a coincidence! The first thoughts that come to my mind are my psychic abilities and I know it for a fact.

31

I knew right away that the nausea that I was experiencing was his. I knew from then on to be more alert for next time I felt something like this.

BRATISLAVA SLOVAKIA / DEC. 2021

CASE NAME: MESSAGE IN THE FLOOR

I was almost done writing my first book and would take walks around town whenever I needed to disconnect from the fucked-up memories. Covid fear was still crippling the city and the mood in town was heavy. Despite the sadness in the air Christmas joy prevailed amongst joyful Christmas food street vendors. In my desperate attempts to disconnect from my book, I found my thoughts engulfed in my new gift.

I tried to make sense of everything that was happening. None of my friends back home or on social media knew what I was going through. It was all so new to me. Most of the psychic readings I didn't remember at all. It was almost like I went into a trance and Ivana had to tell me what I had said.

One day as we sat at home on our couch while Ivana tested my abilities, I suddenly said,

"If I do a psychic reading on a potential new friend, and I cant remember, please don't tell me what I said."

"Why don't you want to know?" she asked.

"I want to get to know people and I don't want them to think that I know their secrets, they may be scared of being my friend." She agreed and asked, "can you read me?"

I looked at the floor tile and I could read her message on the wooden floor. I began to read her mind. It was so weird. We were both in shock. "I can't believe you know what I was thinking!" she yelled out. She jumped up and poured herself a glass of champagne. "How did you do that?"

By now I had already told her how I would see signs all around me, so she walked quickly to the sliding glass door and on to the balcony looking for signs. She looked out at the city then walked in again. She looked around the walls, around the living room, and around where we sat for clues.

"Where did you see the signs?" she asked.

I pointed at the floor.

"I can see the signs on the floor."

She looked down to the floor in disbelief.

"But how can the floor read my mind?"

"I don't know," I answered. I was in disbelief myself.

CASE NAME: I CAN SEE YOUR SKULL

So, remember the neck rash case I wrote about earlier in this book? Well, I still wondered what the message was because it was never clear and was left unfinished.

The celebrity that Ivana had interviewed with, requested that she tattoo him in his home. From time to time she will do this if the tattoo is small and does not require a lot of blood pathogenic drama. She agreed and I thought perhaps I could tap into what it was that his neck rash was telling me while we were there.

We arrived at their home and quickly settled in. I began to speak to his lovely wife as he and Ivana prepared his tattoo design in another room. I was so happy to speak in English with his wife! She spoke in a British accent and was refined, beautiful, and sophisticated.

As she spoke, I connected to her in an unusual way. I loved her dearly and felt a great deal of compassion for her. I wanted to lift her burden.

"You are so tired," I said.

Something greater than me moved me to get up and hug her. It was not a voice it was a feeling. I felt almost like I was picked up from my chair and gently forced over to her to embrace her.

I got up and wrapped my arms around her and said, "You feel so very sad."

She began to cry softly. I did not want to let her go. I embraced her in my arms, and I loved her like I had loved her for so long. I loved her like she was me. As I removed my arms from her body, I looked over in the distance and I could spot a picture of an older man and a baby. It was in a small frame on a shelf, and it was hard to see with my failing vision. Instantly, I knew it was her father's energy that had moved me.

As I struggled to focus in on it, I heard a faint voice say,

"Thank you, thank you for hugging her."

34

HOLY SH*T I'M A F***NG PSYCHIC

"Oh my God!" she said.

"I never cry in front of people!"

"I'm so sorry, this is so embarrassing, but I feel so much better!"

I felt an undeniable type of love and was filled with compassion. I felt a new sense of love energy flowing through me and out of my hands. I looked at her and saw that her face instantly changed, and her sadness had lifted.

Just then, her husband walks in and asks me, "hey listen you said something about my necklace, and you know I don't wear fake shit, so I don't know what you were insinuating by saying that I should take a break from this necklace."

I turned my chair away from them and faced the wall and I began to speak to him. I told him things that only him and I would know. I talked about his business. I talked to him about his fears. And suddenly I could see his skull, like an X ray. Even though I wasn't looking at him, I could see his face, but it was like in an X ray. So that I could only see his skull and the teeth formation. I turned my chair back around to face him. I took one of my hands and cupped it into my upper teeth and the other hand I cupped on my lower teeth and began to pull them apart. Then I started saying ah aah.

He said, "you know those are the sounds that I make when I do my vocal classes with my vocal coach, but I actually stopped those classes a couple of weeks ago." Instantly I knew. I saw the blockage. It was not the necklace. It was a blockage that he had on his vocal cords.

HOLY SH*T I'M A F***NG PSYCHIC

"You need to use your voice for future generations, please do not be afraid anymore. Do it for your daughter. She will have something to be proud of when she looks back to see your lineage. Your lineage will be the message you bring across in your podcast."

"I must confess," he said. "I have been holding back a lot of who I really am because of the treatment that I get from this political regime in our country. I have been afraid to say the things that I would like to say because of the political hold this country has on our freedom of speech."

I encouraged him to continue to speak up for future generations. I can only pray that he does.

CASE NAME: I CAN SEE IT IN HER EARINGS

Every weekend we would drive an hour from Bratislava to Kostolne, a little village about an hour and a half away. Ivana grew up there and her mom still lives there. The village is small surrounded by large fields of dense forest. The air is fresh and life there is extremely quiet.

Ivana's mom welcomed us every Friday evening with a delicious traditional dinner. After dinner, we popped champagne and talked.

This Friday, we could not wait to share my crazy news with Ivana's mom. She immediately asked,

"If you can see these things, can you see any blocks on me?"

HOLY SH*T I'M A F***NG PSYCHIC

I instantly saw her answer in her earrings. I stared at them and began speaking.

"You have trapped energy from your childhood," I said.

"It lays in your hip area."

That is all I knew, so I said,

"I will pray for the answer for you, and it will reveal itself to me when it is time."

During the week, I was stopped in my tracks with her answer.

The next Friday, she was standing by her front gate waiting for us when we went to visit for the weekend. I hugged her and Ivana told her that I had her answer.

We walked inside her home and before we could settle in.

I got behind her and placed one hand over her heart and the other on her back in between her hip bones.

I began to pray and asked God's unconditional love to flow through me.

She stood still and allowed for me to pray over her. Her body was rigid and tense.

I began to speak, and Ivana translated effortlessly.

I told her that her blockages started from the age of five years old.

Her fear of being loved stemmed from the abuse she suffered at the hands of her abusive alcoholic father.

"You have four tall walls around you," I said.

"At around twenty years old, your hardened heart was opened at the beginning of your relationship with your deceased husband."

37

"But your relationship soon fell into a nonromantic pattern that left you bitter and lonely."

"In the end, he viewed you as a sister/companion and without the proper communication tools you were unable to share with him your feelings."

"You never received the love you yearned for, and so, it is now manifesting as pain in your lower back," I said. With my hands still placed over her heart and the other on her lower back between her hips. I prayed silently.

I felt a strong heat come through my hands and on to her lower back as I finished my prayer.

As we jumped into bed later that night Ivana asked,

"How are you doing it?"

"How do you know what to say?"

"How are you so sure that what you're saying is true?"

"I put the bubble of God around me and know that I am just his vessel," I said smiling.

CASE NAME: I KNOW WHAT THEY LOOK LIKE (remote viewing)

We had rented an Airbnb in a high rise in the center of Bratislava. Our unit was comfortable, had a balcony, and overlooked the city. I spent most of my days doing the exact same thing. I made breakfast and lunch for Ivana and walked downstairs and bought myself a baguette to go, then I walked along the Danube River on my gratitude walk. Afterwards I

38

showered and sat down and wrote nonstop until the evening when Ivana got home for dinner.

I was in heaven.

One day, I was busy writing my book when suddenly I got a WhatsApp notification. It was Ivana.

"Can you connect to my client?" she asked.

I stared at the text and immediately took interest in trying to "connect" to her client.

 I had never been to her studio, nor did I have any interest in going there since I was on my sabbatical to write my book.

I put the phone down, stood up, put each one of my hands underneath each one of my armpits, and closed my eyes. With my eyes closed, I felt like I was floating, and I could see into her studio from up above. I moved around effortlessly.

As I floated around, I saw her sitting down tattooing. She was facing her client and he sat facing her. He was tall and skinny and had acne all over his face. I looked over to his side at his mom, who sat next to him.

"He suffers from depression," I texted back to Ivana.

"Something is currently making him very sad, but this message is not for him, it's for his mom."

My armpits began to sweat, and a warm sensation took over my body. I opened my eyes, grabbed my phone and texted:

"Tell his mom, she has to go back to the doctors because she still has lumps under her armpits," I said as I moved my hands around to feel lumps underneath my armpit area.

"Have the doctors check her again."

39

HOLY SH*T I'M A F***NG PSYCHIC

"The cancer is not gone."

I could feel lumps in her armpits. My body shivered.

I focused out of the tattoo studio, and I could see her bedroom.

"Tell her to open up her curtains and let more light in."

"Her bedroom is too dark."

"She needs to move the armoire away from the window and let the natural light in."

I placed my phone on the table and closed my eyes again.

I saw her client's mother's body sitting in a chair in Ivana's studio. I saw what she looked like and how she dressed.

I disconnected from them and continued writing my book.

Ivana picked me up at home after she finished tattooing and we began our hour drive to her mom's village.

"Babe how did you know?" she asked stupefied.

"I don't know babe," I answered.

I told her exactly what I did when her WhatsApp message came through.

"And guess what?" I asked her.

"I know what they looked like!"

I described her client's appearance and said, "his mom was there in the studio with you guys."

"I could see her."

"She is a bigger woman who dressed all in black."

"She has red hair short hair and styled her bangs up with heavy hairspray."

"Yes, babe that is exactly what they looked like. And I never sit opposite of my clients like you described but my client wanted to face me."

CASE NAME: CAN YOU CONNECT TO MY HUSBAND?

We arrived at Ivana's mom's house and quickly sat down for dinner and talked about our week. Ivana translated and I waited patiently to speak. (I believe my psychic ability gets stronger and stronger because of the language barrier; I have been forced to shut the fuck up and be more aware in silence)

Ivana shared with her mom what had just happened, and she turned and stared at me.

"Can you connect with my dead husband?" she asked immediately.

"What the fuck?" I thought.

"I don't know but I can try," I said.

I stared into her eyes and then I began to look around the room. Everywhere I looked, I saw clues and they spoke to me. Suddenly, I began to speak for him.

He said, "I want you guys to remember how fun I was."

"Don't remember me with sadness!"

Suddenly out of nowhere I began to describe details about a couple of trips that only the two of them could know of. I talked about a shell he brought back from a trip to Africa, which he reminded Ivana about. Then, he reminded both about a trip that they took to Hungary. While they reminisced, he asked, "Remember how stinky my feet used to be?"

41

HOLY SH*T I'M A F***NG PSYCHIC

Both Ivana and her mom laughed out loud. Then he talked about how he loved apples and gherkins.

Suddenly, Ivana's mom cried out, "Why did you leave me?"

"Why did you die?"

She stared at me while talking to him. I stared back.

"You left me all alone; you promised you weren't going to give up!" she said holding back her tears.

"I didn't give up!" I heard myself reply.

"I didn't want to die!"

"It came out of nowhere!"

"I wasn't ready for it!"

I then described exactly how he died.

I closed my eyes and looked around. I saw a yellow tiled hospital room.

"I was not ready to die so I kept my mind occupied by counting the tile on the hospital room floor and counted every drop of liquid that poured into my IV."

"I tried to communicate by writing on a notepad with a pencil but by then I was too weak I couldn't write."

"That night, when the sun rose up, I closed my eyes for a few seconds and boom I was dead!"

"Dopiche!" I cried out. (His last words in Slovak)

I could not go back to my body anymore I was dead.

I looked at Ivana's mom's face, she was in complete and utter shock. Then, a smile appeared on her face, and she nodded.

"Yes!"

"This is all true!" "Yes, this is all true!"

HOLY SH*T I'M A F***NG PSYCHIC

"He did have a notepad and pencil and the tile around the rim of the floor in his room was yellow."

Then he disclosed some family secrets that have remained unspoken of since he passed.

"Everyone thinks I was waiting for Peter but no I was waiting to talk to my friend Mirko."

"I wanted to tell him about these secrets."

Ivana's mom then asked if she was doing everything right to keep the house.

"Yes," he said, "but check the rain gutters."

I pointed up towards the corner of the house in the kitchen where we sat.

"Look there," I said.

Ivana's mom smiled and said, "oh everything is ok there, they came two weeks ago to repair the rain gutters, they should be just fine."

Ivana got up to use the restroom and as she left the room, I formed a heart with my hands, and I pointed to Ivana's mom's neck. And I said, "remember the necklace I got for you, do you remember the necklace?

She stared at me. We waited until Ivana returned to translate.

"Yes, I remember it," she replied.

"I still have it; I just haven't worn it for years."

The conversation continued for about 3 hours. They both laughed and carried on. In the end, he said, "I can continue talking all night if you guys want."

HOLY SH*T I'M A F***NG PSYCHIC

By now we were all tired and pretty mind fucked to tell you the truth. We all agreed that we needed time to process what had miraculously happened.

The next day Ivana and I walked out to our car. As I opened the door to climb in, I noticed that the car's rear tire was flat. We proceeded to change the tire when suddenly the rain gutter above us began to leak right on top of Ivana's head. The gutter had a leak that needed to be replaced just like Ivana's dad had said the night before.

CASE NAME: DON'T WORRY, YOUR KIDS WON'T BE LIKE ME

We arrived at a beautiful home ready to celebrate the holidays with one of Slovakia's most famous entertainers, his family, and his friends. I made myself comfortable at the table and proceeded to stuff my mouth with all the delicious food I can possibly get ahold of. It was quite easy since I couldn't join in their conversation. After a while, they all joined me around the table. We all did our best to communicate via Ivana's translation. By now, she was getting better and better at it.

After about 20 minutes of back-and-forth translated convos, I began to get the urge to talk to a certain guy that was at the party. I stuffed my mouth with onion dip over and over to avoid the feeling but eventually the feeling won, and I motioned for him to come sit next to me. He pointed at himself and asked if I was talking to him. I grabbed ahold of Ivana's leg to ensure she stayed by my side to continue to translate.

HOLY SH*T I'M A F***NG PSYCHIC

"Come sit here," I said.

"I have a message from your father," I told him, hoping the onion dip wouldn't start stinking up my breath just yet.

He came and sat next to me without hesitation.

"Yes," he said. "But how?" "My father is dead!" he said smiling.

"Your father wants to apologize for the way he abused you and your mother."

"He wants to admit that his alcoholism took over him and the way he beat you as a child was terrible and unacceptable." "He is so so sorry."

"He is so sorry for how you had to watch him abuse your mother over and over."

"He hopes that you can find it in your heart to forgive him now because he never had the chance to apologize to you when he was alive."

Instantly Niagara Falls took over his eyes and he began to sob. His wife got up off the couch and ran over us to see what the hell was going on.

Someone grabbed a handful of napkins and placed them into his hands to help with the tears, but they just kept flowing.

I watched him weep and felt his pain. The room grew quiet, and we all kept our eyes on him as he gasps for air.

He looked deep into my eyes with his beautiful bright blue eyes now swollen and red and said, "Yes, tell him I forgive him."

"You tell him too, know that his energy surrounds you and guides your step," I said.

"He wants you to know that it is ok to have kids with her."

I looked over at his wife who was now holding him tight.

"He wants you to know that they will not be alcoholics."

"They will not be like him, and you will not be like him either."

"You will be a great dad one day." "It can be now, if you are ready!"

He sobbed again and said, "I've been afraid to have kids because of this."

"We have wanted them desperately, but I held back because of these thoughts always in the back of my mind."

"I have always feared that I would be like my father, so I held back on having a kid."

I looked over at his wife and said, "It is time for a baby."

"Tears rolled down her face instantly."

They both got up and hugged me and thanked me.

CASE NAME: THE PATHOLOGIST

We were at a birthday celebration, and I was exhausted. I usually start crashing around 9 pm.

Around 10:45 I began to feel the pressure of my Spanx and the throbbing of my feet inside my overly expensive shoes that I refuse to ever buy ever again because they always fall apart .

I looked around the party for Ivana with the intention of giving her the "let's go home" stink eye. I had to be careful because she is so innocent that sometimes she just doesn't get the Mexican mom mannerisms I use on her.

HOLY SH*T I'M A F***NG PSYCHIC

I made my way towards the front door and was suddenly stopped by a guy that wanted to show me what he did for a living.

He grabbed my hand and asked, "Can you guess what this is?"

I was so excited, finally I was in front of someone that spoke English. Broken English but at least it was English.

He placed his phone right in front of my face and showed me a picture of a human organ and before I could gag and puke on his shiny iphone13, I blurted out,

"Holy fuck!"

"Excuse me," he said.

"Oh my God," I replied.

"Yes, yes," he said proudly, thinking I was amazed by the picture of a swollen looking piece of raw bloody meat.

"I am so sorry," I said.

He was so proud of himself thinking he had stomped me.

"It's ok," he said.

I grabbed ahold of his shoulder and softly whispered,

"I'm sorry for what happened to you when you were 10 years old."

His jaw dropped.

I looked gently into his eyes and whispered again, "Your brother sexually abused you from the age of 10." "I am so sorry for your suffering."

Immediately his tears began to flow. I watched his screen turn off and his sorrow pour out of his eyes. He grabbed his chest and began to nod.

HOLY SH*T I'M A F***NG PSYCHIC

"Yes," he said.

"Yes, he did, I've carried so much shame for so long and I never told a soul."

"It's time to leave the shame with me I said."

"You have been living your life blaming yourself and everything always feels upside down for you.

"Yes, yes," he said. "I feel upside down." "Exactly."

"Look at your shirt," I said pointing at his upside-down LV. "Even your clothes reflect this!"

His partner came over to us and placed his arms around him and together they cried.

"You need to start downward dog stretching exercises in the mornings and practice yoga this will help to ease you into a life of forgiveness," I said to him.

We were so involved in our conversation and the love of God filled our space that we did not notice that the entire party had come to join us. As I looked back to find Ivana, a line of people waited for their turn.

Suddenly a surge came over me and I started to read and "heal" them one by one.

Happy tears were the main event in this birthday celebration.

CASE STUDY: CRAZY WOMAN

I am normally pretty balanced when it comes to behaving like a little bitch as certain times of the month. I had a hysterectomy a while back and I have been free of PMS since then.

But suddenly, I found myself turning into a raging ball of hormonal emotions. One morning after Ivana left to work, I felt like I could cry and yell at the same time. I wondered if it was because I was beginning to feel deep rooted emotions that had been released while writing my first book. But, deep inside I knew those emotions had been healed a long time ago.

I sat at the table in front of my computer and stared at my reflection on the black computer screen and I prayed.

I closed my eyes, and something told me to go sit on the couch. I sat on the couch and began to hum. I went into a trancelike state. I hummed for over an hour. When I came to, I felt a blessed release and a warm peaceful feeling took over me.

Later that day, I felt the same emotional disruption bubbling inside me, so I quickly went to the couch to hum. From then, every time I felt some weird internal shit, I went into a humming trance and every time I came out, I was filled with peace. This went on for about a week.

CASE NAME: THE LUMP

I joined Ivana at one of her many business meetings at one of my favorite spots on the river walk. My intention was to look pretty and eat and drink while the meeting went on. I pretended to understand and express interest in their discussion. Suddenly Ivana says,

"Yes, Veronica is a psychic."

The guy we met with looks over at me and says,

"Oh, yes!" I believe in that kind of shit!"

"I actually went to this Russian lady who has a monkey that can tell the future!"

"Can you tell me my future?" he asked me, smiling from ear to ear.

"No," I said. "I don't have a message for you!"

"But I have a message for you," I said turning around to face his wife.

I reached out to her and place my hand on her left breast. I touched a lump on her breast. She stared at me with fear.

"You have a lump here that you are very worried about."

"Please stop worrying about it."

"You have nothing to fear, it is just hormonal."

"Nothing will happen to your baby, he is safe"

Her tears rolled out of her eyes.

"How did you know?" she asked.

"Yes, she has been very worried," her husband added.

"She thinks its cancer," he said sadly.

"No!" it is not!" I replied instantly.

"I want you to go home and start doing these humming exercises.

I instantly knew that the feelings I had been having were hers. The humming I had mastered was an exercise meant for her. So, I showed her how to hum through the hormonal changes that her body was going through.

I mimicked the exact breathing exercises I had learned how to do earlier that week.

"Go home and do them every day when you're feeling like you're raging with emotions," I said.

"I feel like that all the time now," she answered.

Weeks later I received a message from her husband that the lump was gone, and her hormones were controlled. Months later her baby was born with no complications.

THE RIDES

Slovakia has a zero-tolerance law on alcohol, so we found ourselves in Uber or Wolt rides 5 days out of the week. For over two months EVERY SINGLE driver got a psychic reading. Every single one of them was receptive and welcomed their reading. Many of them wanted to know more. I gave all of them readings about their families. I never had to look at their face or hear them talk. It was almost as if my psychic abilities had magnified. The psychic readings were quick, starting from the moment we got into the car and ending when we arrived at our location. Ivana got a kick out of everyone because as the interpreter she felt that she was the one with the psychic ability. I loved it.

HOLY SH*T I'M A F***NG PSYCHIC

The following are a couple of memorable ones....

Celine Dion

We got into a taxi one day and Celine Dion's song "My heart will go on" was playing on the radio in a little village about one hour away from Bratislava, the capital of Slovakia. The driver turned it off as we climbed in. I kept singing the song in my head because it had his psychic reading entangled into it. The lyrics to the song brought him a personal message about his worries over his older son. His message also reminded him about his connection to God and brought him hope and peace of mind.

As we got out of the car Ivana asked,

"How did you know all of that?"

"I heard it in the Celine Dion song," I said smiling.

"What the Fuck, the radio was off!" she exclaimed.

"Not in my head!" I answered knowing I couldn't explain it anymore.

Dubai Mom

Ivana gifted me a fantastic trip to Dubai as my birthday present. I wanted to go play in the sands of Dubai's beautiful desert, shop, and eat lavish dinners. I did not expect my psychic abilities to follow me to Dubai, so I was taken back a bit when I gave a psychic reading to the first Uber driver. I got into the car as the cold AC blasted in my face and suddenly my mouth moved. I heard myself giving him a message of love and hope from his mom. He looked at me through the rear-view mirror with disbelief. I looked back at him and said his mom's name in Arabic. Speaking her name in Arabic freaked me out. It felt like I was speaking gibberish. I immediately stopped talking and he did not say a word or look back at me again. I wish now I had kept going perhaps I could have added Arabic as another language in my repertoire.

CALIFORNIA /FEB 2022

I wondered if my psychic abilities would disappear once I arrived in California. I was just getting used to my new calling and life in Europe. I liked myself as a stay-at-home trophy wife and smart as hell self-published author. I enjoyed getting my mind blown every day as a psychic healer and the thought of going home was more foreign than me at a traditional Slovak family gathering. Being tucked away in a small village surrounded by nature brough me so much peace, joy, and fulfillment but because of stupid immigration laws, I was kicked out of the European union.

I love America, don't get me wrong but landing in Los Angeles was a total shit show, and I could feel instant internal stress before we even landed. I took a couple of days off before returning to work to allow me time to adjust.

CASE NAME: LILAC MEMORIES

On our second day back, Ivana and I jumped into the service elevator and headed out for our gratitude walk. The elevator doors opened, and the ripe smell of doggy accidents welcomed us in. We looked at each other and both hoped we could hold our breaths long enough to make it down thirty-three floors. A shy middle-aged woman stood in the corner opposite us. She held on to a couple of large bags and a white wire rack of some sort.

I looked at her and my heart hurt for her loneliness, I loved her. Suddenly my big mouth blurts out,

"Your mom says hi!"

"Shit!" I smelled the horrible elevator smell instantly.

I glanced at Ivana, and she still held her breath.

The lady in the elevator answered,

"My mom is dead."

"I know!" I answered.

"Your mom still says hi," I said.

The lady looked at me and turned back away trying hard not to roll her eyes.

"She wants me to tell you that her favorite color was lilac," I said.

"Yes," she answered. Smiling from ear to ear.

She turned her body to face me.

All of a sudden, her eyes weren't rolling anymore, and she was ready for more.

I only wish I left her hanging. (Just kidding!)

HOLY SH*T I'M A F***NG PSYCHIC

"She wants you to talk to her on your drive home."

The ding of the elevator doors shocked us both and a desperate dog and its owner wabbled in. (I could feel the dog's energy. I knew it wanted to pee so bad. Poor thing was locked indoors all day.)

I took my eyes off the dog and said, "You have about two hours of conversation, don't you?"

"Yes, I have quite the drive," she said.

"I'm driving back to San Diego."

"Enjoy the talk," I said.

"I will," she smiled and walked out of the elevator.

I looked at Ivana, she was still holding her breath but was ready to burst.

As we walked out of the building, her car almost ran us over as she waved goodbye at me with excitement.

I smiled at the lilac bumper sticker on her car.

Ivana and I looked at each other. She smiled wickedly and said, "I think you know your psychic gift is still here!"

HOLY SH*T I'M A F***NG PSYCHIC

CASE NAME:
HOW THE HELL AM I GOING TO TELL MY FRIENDS?

I went for my gratitude walk on the beach and ventured as close as I could to the ocean water. I watched dolphins swimming in the distance and an overwhelming joy took over me. I must admit, it was nice to be back on the dirty sands of Long Beach. I could not help to be grateful for how far I had come from the crystal meth addict that once ran high as fuck on these sands hoping that no one would talk to her.

I gathered my thoughts and quickly changed my vibration. Instead, I planned my dinner menu in my head. (Whenever I run, I like to prepare food menus in my head and try them as experiments.) I was super excited because I had planned to cook an elaborate dinner for my friends that evening and could not wait to see how it would end up.

As I mentally reviewed my shopping list, I could not help but wonder, "how the hell am I going to tell my friends that I am a psychic?" Last time they saw me I was not only hot, but I was the best permanent makeup artist in the world. In fact, I had not even written my first book yet. They probably thought I would brag about how it went to #4 on Amazon's New Hot Releases or talk about how accomplished I felt to be the publisher and editor. They had no clue what they were in for.

I asked God to fill my filthy mouth with the proper words so that I did not scare the shit out of them. I did not care too much about how I would sound or if I looked like a fool because I am hot so looking like a fool never really bothers me.

HOLY SH*T I'M A F***NG PSYCHIC

As I prayed, I had a vision of how it would go down.

Joe would be speechless, and Frank would lean back into his chair. (I know it would feel fantastic because the chairs are new, and they are fabulous – took us six months to get, after Covid everything was delayed- we all know the story)

Frank would then cross one arm over his stomach and with the other one, he would reach his hand over his mouth. Then, he would ask,

"Well, Veronica, do you have something psychic to tell me?"

Before I could see anything else, I heard a voice saying,

"Tell Frank I don't like where he put my picture."

In my mind, I saw a woman in a blue dress. I instantly knew it was Frank's wife who had passed way before I met him. I had never seen her in real life, but my soul knew it was her.

"Tell him its dark and I don't feel celebrated."

"I celebrate them, please celebrate my memory."

I smiled and made my way back to our tiny ass kitchen and cooked everything on one pan using only my one knife. (That's a whole other story but I should confess – in this little kitchen, I only have one knife and one pan and IDGAF)

As soon as they arrived, we sat at the dinner table. (New too by the way, took us six months to get, after Covid everything was delayed- we all know the story)

They caught us up with all of their news and we celebrated them over champagne.

Before the beef wellington made its debut, I spilled the beans, not as an appetizer but as the tea.

HOLY SH*T I'M A F***NG PSYCHIC

Their eyes popped open, and Joe was speechless. Just as I had envisioned and almost on cue, Frank leaned back into his chair, placed his arms and hands as I had envisioned them and asked, "Well, Veronica, do you have something psychic to tell me?"
"Well, as a matter of fact, I fucking do!" I said.
I went ahead and told him everything his wife had told me to tell him.
His eyes grew big with my every word. His jaw dropped when I finished.
Then I turned to Joe and began to unleash with the outmost gentle care.
"You have been having suicidal thoughts and they have begun to take over"
As I spoke, I heard myself speaking and could not believe it. This was a man I had known for almost a decade and never knew this about him.
I looked at him and my eyes felt deep empathy and I loved him. I loved him for the first time. Like I was just seeing him for the first time in my life.
His eyes filled quickly with tears, and they flowed effortlessly and freely down his face, onto his beard and then onto his shirt. His body was covered in sweat as he began to sob. (It took a long time for the tears to reach his body because his beard is so damn thick – he is a bear and bears need thick beards – but non the less they did make it down eventually.)
He looked deep into my eyes and said,
"Yes."

58

HOLY SH*T I'M A F***NG PSYCHIC

His glanced moved onto Frank then to Ivana and then back to me.
"I believed that I would kill myself this past Tuesday!"
"What!" Frank yelled out.
We all got up and held him. We embraced each other as minutes went by. I held him as if he were dead. I could not imagine the idea of his passing. It would shatter us all.
We all cried together and soon he breathed a sigh of relief.
"I feel so much lighter," Joe said.
"Thank you for bringing this to light."
After they left, I thanked God for my psychic gift.

CASE NAME: THE CARPENTER

I arrived in my tattoo studio and felt like I was visiting a past life. The walls were extra white, and the light felt harsh and synthetic. The floors were dusty, and the glass windows showed proof of tiny little inquisitive humans that had been peering in leaving their filthy little paw prints behind. I instantly turned-on high frequency sounds and began to set up my workstation.
My client came in for me to touch up her lip tattoo in the middle of my meditation. I felt so out of touch with reality.
As I began to touch her, I felt her father energy.
"Was your father a carpenter?" I asked carefully. Hoping not to weird her out.
"No." she replied instantly.

"Ok, I thought, maybe my psychic gift is gone, and I lost my touch." (I was always thinking my psychic ability would miraculously disappear just as quickly as it had appeared.)

I backed off and instead of proving that her father was indeed a carpenter I talked about life. Unable to talk, she relaxed into her lip tattoo. Then, a message came in from her father. As I let go of her lip, she said, "actually, you know what Veronica, my father did get into carpentry after he retired."

I finished her tattoo and sat in silence after she left. I turned off the lights in my studio and traced back the entire conversation. I slowly began to understand just a little bit of what happened to me when Spirit spoke through me.

In the silence I heard a voice inside that said,

"Trust yourself, trust your gut, it is your intuition. It is all the same. It is all from God."

CASE NAME: JESSIE

We joined our friends in Catalina Island to celebrate their birthdays. As we sat at the Yacht Club their friends joined our table. Ivana and I introduced ourselves and soon the conversation turned into a talk about their friend who had suddenly passed away.

"Is there a Jesus or Jessi?" I asked the lady that told us of his passing.

"Yes," she said.

"His daughter's name is Jessi. She is the one that is taking it the hardest."

60

"Please tell her, that he is sorry for keeping his illness from the family. Tell her that he did not want to burden them, and, in all honesty, he did not know how to deal with it himself. He really did not believe he would die so suddenly."

"Please tell her that he loves her and will always be with her," I said.

She looked deep into my eyes and said, "yes, he kept it from his family and yes I will tell her."

"Thank you for your words, I believe in this kind of stuff."

CASE STUDY: DRUNK VERONICA (ME)

As we settled into our California bullshit life again and got back into our social environments, I began to see that the more I drank the more psychic I became. I mean, give me an extra glass of champagne or an extra dirty martini and I could get down to the persons' most hidden secrets and reveal the color under the color under the color of the paint in their house.

But, the next day, I honestly did not feel good about it. For the most part, I would black out about the psychic reading and not remember any of it. And most of all I just did not feel good because it felt like an intrusion.

Even though I always had Ivana to tell me what had happened, I felt like I was showing off or doing it for laughs or on an ego trip. It simply did not feel good if I was drinking.

One day, as we sat around the bar at one of our local favorite restaurants a couple of guys sat next to us. By now, I was a little

61

tipsy. I tapped one of the guys on his shoulder and said, "hey your great uncle wants to say hi!"

He looked at me and rolled his eyes. "We are brothers," the guy next to him said as he reached out his hand to shake mine. "Are you a psychic?" he asked. "Our sister is also a psychic."

Then his brother turned around and faced me. "What is my great uncles name?" he asked.

"His name is Jorge." I made sure to pronounce his name in Spanish.

"Oh, you speak Spanish too or is that also one of your superpowers?" he asked.

"Listen, first of all, all Mexicans have an uncle named Jorge and second of all, I don't give two shits about what you think my uncle Jorge wants to say to me!" "So, thanks but no thanks!"

He waved goodbye in my face as he swiveled his barstool turning his back on me forcefully.

His brother's faced popped over behind his back and mouthed, "I'm sorry, he's having a difficult day!"

My eyes filled with tears, and I swallowed a lump in my throat. I quickly blinked to avoid crying and Ivana rubbed my back.

"Are you ok?" she asked.

"Don't take it personal, that guy has issues you can tell from a mile away."

First of all, I am Mexican, and I don't have an uncle named Jorge and second of all I have never been dissed like that!

I quickly sobered up. As I drank water, I imagined the cup was filled with shame. I drank it down and asked for the check.

HOLY SH*T I'M A F***NG PSYCHIC

"I need silence for a bit," I said as jumped into our Uber.

"What the fuck was that?" I asked God.

"Don't throw your pearls to the swine and stop acting a fool," I heard God's voice loud and clear.

From then, I began to hoan in on my psychic gift. I did not abuse it. I did not really share the news about my new gift with anyone that gave me bad vibes. I held it close to my heart and honored it. I began to get very choosy with whom I shared news of my new psychic ability that no one around me really knew what was going on in my life. Not even some of my closest colleagues or friends.

It was hard at first, because I touched people every day. I tattooed faces and intimate parts of the body for a living. So, when I would touch a client, instantly I would either have a message of love and hope or I would know their blocks and how to heal them. I would know intimate parts of their life and that of those around them. I struggled with this, should I tell her or should I not tell her on a daily basis.

I began to take inventory of the times that my intuition knew things. I began to recall all of the times when I just simply knew not to trust or who to trust.

I remembered the time when Ivana and I were traveling to Iceland and enjoyed our layover in Germany. I had a psychic reading for many strangers who passed by me. I knew their name and each and every one of their story. We found it to be hysterically funny and were amused by my stories for about an hour. But, looking back, I just knew it was my psychic ability all along. I just don't think I was ready to accept it.

CASE NAME: MARGARET

Every other month we live in Montecito for a week. We have a great Hawaiian / Mexican family there that love us with pure hearts and clean energy. We vibrate high and always attract magic.

A couple of years ago, they graciously invited us to work out of their luxury med spa. I quickly gathered a great clientele base there and Ivana and I feel as if we are home.

As soon as we could get up there, we did. We gathered around their kitchen counter and shared delicious food and drank champagne. The times in their home are my most favorite. We shared our news with them, and they celebrated us with great joy.

The next day, as I walked into their med spa, my body knew that the energy there was different. I could feel a high vibration. As I prepared for my client, I asked God to use me.

As I worked on my second client both her and I knew that something special was about to happen. She shared her life story with me, and I shared some of mine with her. I told her about my book, and she said she would someday write one too. As I stretched her eyelid to tattoo her eyeliner, I asked "Who is Margaret?"

64

HOLY SH*T I'M A F***NG PSYCHIC

I pulled my tattoo machine away from her eye just in time for her to quickly yell out, "that is my mom." Then she added she is the woman who became my mom after my mom died."

"Your mom wants to thank her."

"Please tell her how much she appreciated her for taking such great care with you."

"She wants you to know that she did love you, but her mental illness got in the way of many things."

Before I could go on, her tears began to flow.

A personal message of love and hope followed leaving their souls free of guilt, questions, and trauma.

After, I finished her eyeliner tattoo we hugged goodbye, and she thanked me. I closed the door and turned off the lights. I stood in the procedure room holding myself. I was mind fucked.

Months later, she drove down to my Long Beach studio to see me.

"I told my mom Margaret," she said smiling. "She was tickled to hear about my session with you," she said.

"Please remind me about that session," I said hoping she would tell me it was all a dream or in my imagination.

Time stood still as she went over the miracle of that day. Everything I remembered was true.

CASE NAME: AURORA

My next client waited patiently for her anesthetic to take effect for me to tattoo her brows. I tattooed her in the stillness of a guided meditation that played in the background. Suddenly, I felt an energy peeking in the door. I glanced over to see who it was as sometimes people like to peek in on me as I work. But to my surprise there was no one there. Again, it happened and again I looked.

Finally, I heard a woman's voice say, "Aurora."

I asked my client, "Do you know an Aurora?"

"No," she said.

This happened repeatedly throughout the day so I knew that energy had a message for someone I would see.

At the end of the day, I asked my last client if she knew an Aurora. Her body quickly tensed up and her eyes grew wide with fear.

"Yes," she said softly.

Before she could finish, I said, "She has been here all day, waiting for you to come to see me."

"She wants to apologize to you for the way she treated you."

"Yes, she was very, very mean to me when she was alive."

"She was a cold brutal woman; she was my mother-in-law."

A private message of love and hope followed, and my client was able to make peace with their relationship.

THE FIRST FEATHER

Soon after we returned from Montecito, I woke up to Ivana staring at me. Instead of hearing Ivana's every day, "Dobre rano," I heard, "Babe, how many appointments do you have this month?"

I quickly realized it was about that time of the year when she gets the "lets fuck off to the middle of nowhere to the farthest part of the planet on a wild adventure" mindset.

The only reason I considered to entertain her next question before she even asked me is because our condo was involved in a shit storm of LA bullshit never ending renovations.

"I have a full schedule or not that many appointments this month, it depends on why you're asking," I said.

"Do you want to fuck off from this renovation nightmare and go somewhere with me?"

"When?" I asked hoping she would think twice.

"As soon as you reschedule all your clients," she said smiling from ear to ear.

It was Friday morning and by that evening my monthly schedule was cleared of all work responsibilities and we were drinking champagne staring at the world map.

"I think we should go here," she said pointing her tattoo carbon paper-stained fingernail at a remote island off the coast of Tahiti.

I looked at all my clothes piled high on our new furniture in the living room and through the half missing wall into our bedroom and said,

HOLY SH*T I'M A F***NG PSYCHIC

"Ok, let's get the fuck out of this shit hole!"
By Sunday morning we were off the grid.
Our souls soared in high vibration energy as we toured several islands. We took in the energy from every remote corner of the jungles. We ate fruit from the jungle floors, and I touched everything I could so I could pick up on its energy. We swam in shark infested waters without a care and laid on white sandy unexplored beaches for hours. We toured around the high mountains in the back of a pick-up truck and let the islands heavy rain soak our designer clothes beyond recognition. We over dozed on local fish, coconuts, and on violet lilac skies. Every day was magic.

One day, while we explored the jungle in Nuku Hiva, our guide stopped the truck to pick a local flower and gave us a taste of ripened guava. Mexico memories flooded my brain as I bit into the guava, and I closed my eyes to take it all in. When I opened my eyes, I saw a black feather.
I stared at it and heard a voice that instructed me to pick it up.
"Pick it up!"
"Hurry, pick it up!"
I glanced away then looked back at the long black feather.
"You'll regret it."
"Pick it up," I heard the voice again.
I stopped chewing and quickly wondered, "is this guava some kind of ayahuasca shit?"
Because, firstly, I am completely deaf in that ear, so I thought I was beginning to get high of the guava and hearing shit.

HOLY SH*T I'M A F***NG PSYCHIC

Secondly, I am not a feather girl, nor do I pick up random shit and take it home as a "souvenir".

(Unless it's my first time in Rome and it's a twenty-five-pound ancient street cobblestone – then I do pick it up and smuggle it back to America in my suitcase – but that's another story)

"Ivana, pick up that feather for me!" I blurted out.

She looked at me and asked, "why do you want that?"

"Just get it, hurry," I said as our tour guide motioned her to get back into our truck.

I cared for the feather all the way back to Long Beach, not knowing why or what it would come to mean.

Since that day I began picking up every black feather that brutally interrupted my path. Especially those that were blatant. Soon, I had a large collection and each feather represented something. (More later in the book)

Later, I found out that my Aztec ancestors used feathers in their shaman sessions. It made me smile.

HOLY SH*T I'M A F***NG PSYCHIC

TIME TO MEDITATE

Out of nowhere, I kept hearing, "Veronica, it's time for you to meditate." I heard it as soon as I woke up and through out the day. Then I remembered about my time with Tara.

About two years ago, a lady walked into my Long Beach studio. I normally keep my door locked but for some reason, that day, I accidently left it unlocked.

I was on my way to the restroom when I heard, "Are you Veronica?"

"Yes, that's me," I said.

"I was referred to you about permanent eyeliner."

I needed to pee so badly and wished I had locked the door. I stared at the keys hanging from the keyhole on the front door.

"Yes," I said again.

"I wanted to know if you would be interested in trading services instead of money as payment?"

(I have done this with hairstylist, massage therapists, estheticians, etc. – I believe it is good business karma)

"Yes," I said again.

"Yes, she exclaimed seeming a bit shocked that I said yes again.

"Take my card and text me, I will respond with my availability."

I handed her my business card and hoped the conversation was over.

I squeezed my legs as tight as I could and hoped she would leave before I peed myself, but she did not.

"Well, don't you want to know what I do?" she asked.

70

HOLY SH*T I'M A F***NG PSYCHIC

"What do you do?" I asked hoping it would be a short job description.

It was not short, and I did not understand a word she said. All I heard was Marisa something and acupuncture.

"Ok, maybe Ivana can try it," I said. This time, I placed my hand behind her and walked her out the door.

She did text me later and it turned out that she did RTT. (AKA past life regression therapy)

Ivana went crazy for it. She knew all about Marisa Peer's teachings and could not wait to try it.

We both went together to our separate sessions. Long story short because this is supposed to be a booklet not a book, we both had some real cool shit come through. (Ivana can tell you about her experience in her book.) In my session, I experienced my own death as a blind woman and my rebirth. During my birth, I experienced the aurora borealis and comforted myself as I wept and released trapped trauma. In the end, and before my birth, Spirit said "your words are like colors here! Your words are like colors here." I repeated that over and over. Then, Spirit instructed me to meditate for an hour a day.

Some crazy shit! Right? Like, come on what the fuck is that? Who makes this up?

If it didn't happen to me, I would say the person writing this book was high on crack or a mental case. (Actually, I was once on drugs and a mental case, but that story is in my second book and that is not the case now.)

HOLY SH*T I'M A F***NG PSYCHIC

Fast forward to about a year later. I had forgotten the part about meditating for an hour; Or maybe I chose to dismiss it because the entire experience was so liberating but super weird that I filed it under "save for later."

Now, suddenly, I found myself longing to meditate. I was craving a feeling I never felt before. I pulled up my recorded session and listened to it over and over for several days. Until, early one day, I made my way into the living room and youTubed a guided meditation.

I ventured into a world of meditation that I never knew of. Yes, living in California you hear that word all the time, just like vegan, yoga, organic, etc. All that fake social media shit all blends in together after a while. So, I assumed that meditation was just as fake as social media was.

I began to meditate for about an hour a day for over a month and it blew my mind. My body knew what to do almost like it had been meditating my whole life. I began to try different poses and used different methods of breathing. It was like I had a personal meditation instructor download instructions into my head the night before. I quickly began to write them down just in case I went crazy. That way, the meditations would be to blame.

The following are several of the most surreal and memorable meditations that took place in our little condominium in Long Beach. I did not edit them much, (I do not edit much to begin with) I left them as raw as when I initially recorded them,

72

because I was on such a high when I came out from them. I hope you can feel my energy when reading them.

THE FREAKING MEDITATIONS THAT ROCKED MY WORLD!

MEDITATION NAME: SPACE TRAVEL

I started floating up into the universe and then, I looked down and looked down on the planet. I saw the planet's breathtaking beauty. Then I started floating up into the universe. Then, I floated into a gratitude state. Then, everything was dark, and I couldn't see anything. I just started thanking God for everything. I knew I was in the universe, but I couldn't see so instead of trying too hard to focus, I just started thanking God for everything. Thank you so much, thank you so much for my life, my Ivana, my job, my friends, my home, my life, my everything, a sense of gratitude overflowed in my body and suddenly, I could see Saturn. I was floating like an astronaut. I was floating like a satellite, floating by. I felt like my eyes were opened and I saw the hole, the big round circle and realized that it was Jupiter. Then I quickly floated back by Saturn. Then, I saw Mars glowing orange and then I saw Venus. I then looked for Neptune because I wanted to see its beautiful blues. Then suddenly, I was out, out of the Milky Way. I looked back and I could see the Milky Way. It was beautiful, ah, so very beautiful and white. Then I was up and so far, away, then I took my guide's hand, and we entered a portal.

I saw myself surrounded by a pure white light. I could feel the light's energy. I could feel it wrap around me like a cloak of protection and could feel its energy enter my body and it filled me with pure light. I was part of the energy, and the energy was part of me. The energy was pure love.

I saw myself in a flower field and the fragrance of the flowers filled me with joy. I felt at home. My sanctuary. I felt safe, loved, and protected. Always.

I saw a mystique shape taking form. My beautiful spirit guides. I felt a smile form on my human face, and I placed my hand in their hand. I floated high above the Planet into the Milky Way. I moved fast. It was beautiful. I came upon a glowing portal of light. I felt excited.

I looked into a mirror and saw myself, my reflection. It was ever knowing and calming. I was in a white robe and my hair was flowing.

MEDITATION NAME: SHAMANIC JOURNEY

I laid on the floor and closed my eyes. I walked into a beautiful Native American dance. All my elders welcomed me and looked at me with great pride and joy. I sat down next to them around ancient stones that held a fire.

Indigenous music and ancient vocals led me into a meditative trance. I ventured into the center of the Earth, and it was dark. I was not scared. I walked into an ancient firepit and danced around it several times. I jumped into the center of the fire landing on my back.

HOLY SH*T I'M A F***NG PSYCHIC

I asked my ascended masters for help with my psychic abilities. I opened my legs and shot fire from my vagina. I released all the doubt and questions I had about my psychic and healing abilities. Then, I saw six ancient faces looking down on me. Three on each side.

Then I heard, "we are all with you," and I looked up and saw millions of stars. Then the stars began to spin and formed a pentagon. The pentagon shape was empty. I then saw everything turn to aqua blue.

I heard soft native sounds that went louder and louder. I came out of meditation to the beat of loud drums and soft flutes.

MEDITATION NAME: SPIRIT GUIDE

I closed my eyes, and I was up and so far, away, then I took my guide's hand, and we entered a portal.

I heard a voice instruct my guide to gently guide me, but instead my guide pushed me in. I flew into the portal, and everything was velvet, red velvet, everything was red velvet. And I was like "Oh my gosh this is so royal." Then I felt a voice say, "you are royal! "You are royal!"

Everything was velvet. Then, I walked into a billion gardens and all the trees and the plants and everything there was all red velvet. Then, I turned around and all the buildings were all red velvet. I looked up into the heavens and all the birds flying by were all red velvet, everything was red velvet.

I walked slowly into a massive room, and it was all mother of pearl. All the walls, the floors, the furniture, the plants, the curtains-everything mother of pearl. Beautiful! Then I walked into a golden room. It was covered in golden picture frames. In the pictures I saw all my lifetimes. I touched each picture of me in every lifetime. I could see me, and I understood each lifetime. I recognized me in each picture. I looked down the wall and it went on into infinity. I wanted to touch all my lifetime picture frames but I couldn't see the end. The wall of pictures went up and I was able to float in through the space of time. I was able to float to the front but then it just expanded and kept going and going. I let go of my need to see my pictures and floated, and floated, and floated but I was still there.

Then, I turned around and I saw all the rooms and I saw the big golden light coming out from underneath one of the doors. I knew to pick that one, so I went there, and everything was gold everything was covered in gold. All the paintings, the walls, the floor, everything was gold. There was a table in the center, it was marble with a white candle in the middle. I walked closer and as I focused in; I saw the keeper. It had a male energy; it was a blob. Weird thing, I could see him as a blob but also as a man. When it saw that I was able to see that, he began molding into a man then into a blob then back into a man. I dropped on my face and began to be grateful with this nonhuman gratitude. I was thanking him, and I just started crying and thanking him. We didn't communicate. I finished being grateful and was flooded with questions. Am I on the right path? Am I psychic? Am I not? Was I imagining? What is all of this? Am I going to be used more? Am I going to be able to heal people? Will I be able to do this for the rest of my life? What is it that I want to do? Am I going to be speaking? All these questions started coming out and I recognized them as fears, but they were just flowing, flowing, flowing out.

And then my body started singing. This weird voice started singing but they were questions, my sounds were questions, almost like I was speaking in tongues. After I finished, I just began to be grateful again and I did not hear anything. Then he leaned in, and he kissed my cheek, and I just lost it. I began to sing like ooh, ooh like howling singing. These beautiful sounds, beautiful in my ear. I couldn't tell if I was loud or if I was screaming. I don't know what it is but, in my ear, it sounds beautiful harmonious like music of the harp. So beautiful and that just made me lose it again. I molded into a blob of gratitude.

Then I started to disconnect. My mind was like this shit is too weird. I started to cut out. I didn't want to see more. It was overwhelming. I laid on the golden ground and just when I was going to get up, they said, "no, don't go anywhere." Stop, relax, relax, be quiet, be quiet." Then I got the feeling to sing ahhhhh.

I started hearing all the answers coming in like big crystals, you know like crystals underneath the planet. I was surrounded by stalactites; they were glowing white. I started feeling like the crystals were coming into my mouth and they were all the answers. They slowly formed into my mouth, and I started going ahhhhh, aaaah, aaaaaah.

I could hear them saying, "open wide, open wide, open wide!" I could feel that those crystals were coming in my mouth, but they were answers to my questions. And then, in the end I thanked them. I could hear a screeching sound like "EEEEEE". I could hear EEEE coming out of my voice. In the end, I was a blob of peace, and I felt unconditional love. I started telling them "I love you; I love you; I love you; I love you; I love you; I love you!" I just became quiet for a couple of minutes and then my meditation was over.

MEDITATION NAME: ACCESS AKASHIC RECORDS

As soon as I close my eyes, gigantic ancient tree roots grow out rapidly from inside and out through my feet. They fly out our condo sliding glass doors, fly into the Villa Riviera, then down into the planet Earth. My roots then wrapped themselves all over the planet. They then grew into the universe flying to a distant planet millions of years away. I then saw roots from my arms grow out rapidly. First one grew out going way past Catalina Island and all the way out into the distance. I then saw it wrapped around Venus. My head then opened, and roots came flying out too. I heard the sound of the roots like they were breaking rock. I took a deep breath and had to calm myself down. My heart was raising fast. I went back into darkness and instead I focused in on the sounds of the meditation. I felt overwhelmed. After a few breaths, I felt ready to continue.

I was floating in the outer space, and I was wrapped around ultraviolet liquid water. I did not feel human. I was just energy.

HOLY SH*T I'M A F***NG PSYCHIC

Then I saw myself standing here next to me. I was floating next to my bed looking down on myself meditating. I was energy so I made my human body levitate. When I saw this, I freaked out, so I went back to the sounds of my meditation. I then focused on the vast darkness. It was overwhelming again. I took a couple of deep breaths and dove right back into the meditation.

I entered into this space, and I was a beautiful ginormous being of light with angel wings that dropped all the way back. They dragged on the floor; it was beautiful! I knew it was me, but I knew that my body was here, on Earth because I could see myself still laying meditating on the bed.

I could feel another version of me. I walked and met up with this creature. He came and looked at me. I thought he was Egyptian. I recognized him to be one of those human Gods with the bird head and the bird beak. I looked at him and he looked at me. We looked past each other's eyes, and I could see love and kindness. He looked at me and he didn't talk. He told me through his eyes, "all of the answers will come through your eyes!" "All of your answers will come through your eyes!" Then I looked on the side and there was this big hole in a rock. It was round and I went in there and I jumped into it and into a big body of light.

I was flying through outer space to all the stars and then I walked into a library full of golden stacks of gold books. The books were so very heavy, and my wings were so light like a bunny feather. I cannot describe the lightness. They were so light and beautiful, yet I was able to pick up these heavy books.

HOLY SH*T I'M A F***NG PSYCHIC

I opened one and it was mother of Pearl again. I ran my wing over the pages, and I could read the words because they were Braille. But they were Braille from antiquity. It wasn't human Braille. It was figures almost like Egyptian figures.

Then I started asking the book questions about my purpose. I already knew the answer and I also understood the book. In the book, I read, "you are chosen, you will because I am."

I heard my human brain think, "Am I really psychic?" "Do I have psychic abilities?" Then they (the book) said, "yes, you do." Then, I picked up another book and I opened it. It was flowing with blood and the blood got all over my wings. Then number seventy-six came into awareness, and it was a message that felt like, "you were born with it, it's in your blood from 1976." The pages of the book then turned into blood. And I could flip the blood with my wings.

I came back to my body because it was too much for me to handle. My heart was raising and then I started shaking, it felt electrifying. I took deep breaths and went back into meditation.

I saw Veronica, my body electrocuting in bed, but I wasn't afraid that it would die.

Then I asked another question, and I could see my human body get up out of bed. It went to the other side of the closet, and it showed me new dresses that I bought. And they (the books) said "just like these dresses that are new with the tags here in your closet, they do not become you until you wear them." "You must step into your power!"

HOLY SH*T I'M A F***NG PSYCHIC

A white dress floated out of the closet, and I heard them say, "When you wear this dress it becomes you, when you step into your power it becomes you." "Wear your powerful psychic gifts with pride!" "Accessorize them wear them!"

Then I asked more and more questions and I knew the answer before the question was formed into my human brain. It was so intense the questions kept coming and the answers kept coming.

MEDITATION NAME: OPEN CROWN CHAKRA

I burned some Palo Santo, grabbed my black feather, and placed it on my forehead. I slid on my eye mask and placed my headphones over my ears. I drifted on into a complete relaxed meditative state. I saw a deep, deep, deep green color. I felt a fear on the right side of my body. I grew deep roots like the ones I saw in Nuku Hiva. I grew the roots all the way down except this time I stopped at the beach, and I put my roots into the ocean. The roots dragged me into the deep blue sea. I told the whales that I was afraid and all of a sudden, several whales came and surrounded my roots and protected me. But I still feared until they started bringing their babies into my roots; and cradling their babies on my roots and surrounding all my roots. Then more and more whales came and surrounded every inch of my roots. I was able to be at peace and the fear disappeared. I then was able to focus on each chakra. When I got to my heart chakra, I began to weep, and I began to tell myself, "I love you, I love you, I love you, I love you." "Little girl, I love you little girl."

HOLY SH*T I'M A F***NG PSYCHIC

When I got to my throat chakra, I started making these weird Native American sounds, wooo, wooo, iiii, woo heeee woooo heeee wooo haaaaa heeeee heeee Hooooo haaa heeee heeee.
 Suddenly my body started shaking rapidly and I felt electricity behind the back of my head. I felt a tingling. I then moved up to my crown chakra and my head started shaking back and forth. I took a deep breath after a while and let my body do whatever I needed to do.

And then, I saw this beautiful massive Lotus flower on top of my head, and I became the Lotus flower. The lotus bulb was under water and the flower was floating on top of the ocean. Suddenly, the whales came and with their tail started splashing water on top of my Lotus petals repeatedly. After a bit, I levitated off the water and flew up into the atmosphere like a fire from the sun all while liquid water dripped down. It was so intense. I disconnected. I took a couple of moments to breathe, and I ran to the restroom, and I had a massive case of diarrhea. I came back to my bed and my black feather was on my pillow.

MEDITATION NAME: MEET MY SPIRIT ANIMALS

I woke up early and ventured into the living room. The city felt quiet, and the light of the morning sun just barely lit up the sky. I laid down on our new carpet, covered myself, and breathed in the new carpet smell. By now my meditation state was almost robotic, it felt so familiar like I had been doing it for centuries. I started my meditation with the sound of Indigenous drumming. I closed my eyes and quickly flew into the universe. I flew past

HOLY SH*T I'M A F***NG PSYCHIC

Saturn and into an endless sea of stars. I could see three heads on either side of me, six in total. I knew they were my guides.

I then walked into the jungle in Nuku Hiva. I am wearing a white dress and I am walking barefoot through historical ancient ruins. The smell of guava fills my nose with pleasure. I walked towards a pool of water located towards the end of a large field. I look over in the distance behind me and see a wild horse that Ivana had played with while on our trip there. A reindeer joined him. The reindeer approached me ever so tenderly. His face was freckled.

I continue walking towards the pool of water and investigate it. It is very deep but small, almost like the size of a jacuzzi. It is surrounded by ancient stones.

I gently step over the stones and turn my back towards the water, I push off with my feet and glide into the pool. My back gently floats on the water. I stare into the vastness of trees up above me. I then become aware that there is a Toucan that sits on the rocks that line the sides of the pool. He watches out for me. Never looking at me. The deer and the horse walk closer to me. As I stare into the beautiful forest of intertwined tree branches above me, I watch a few swallows circle above me. Then a bunch of monarch butterflies circle my head area. Then I become aware of a black jaguar that glides down a tree near me. It watches inquisitively at everything that is going on.

I thank them and gently come out of my meditation session.

MEDITATION NAME: RISE OF THE PHOENIX

I laid on the couch with my back on the seat and my legs on the back rest and onto the wall. I felt my head flood with a rush of blood as I slowly drifted into the sound of Indigenous drums. I walked through the darkness and into a fire pit. Then, I became the fire. I danced as the fire to the rhythm of Indigenous vocals in a meditation that lasted about an hour.

I heard the elders talk to me about self-love. They talked in different languages, but I understood them. Their voices were so beautiful.

They told me not to be afraid, I have always had this gift.

As I came out of the fire, I floated upwards. I saw myself from above the earth. I watched as I laid upside down on the couch and marveled at the phoenix that rose out of me into the day.

As I slowly came out of my meditation, I flipped my body into a sitting position. I had been frozen for over an hour.

*I decided then, I would invest in myself and get a speaking coach to help me speak in public. I had been struggling to sign the contract she had emailed me. I tend to always give so much to others but never invest in myself for my own growth. I printed the contract at work. Ivana recycles paper at work and guess what was on the back of my contract? A phoenix!

Synchronicities began to rule my every day and messages began to get clearer and cleared. I felt more and more secure with my new calling.

The work that usually took me two hours to finish, was taking forty-five minutes to complete and I felt free to grow into something else.

A MEETING WITH MY GUARDIAN ANGEL -ALFIN

By now I began to feel an overwhelming sensation prior to my meditations. They were so fucking wild, and each one more intense than the previous one. I began to ask myself if I had the strength to go into my meditations. For heaven's sake, I thought they were supposed to be relaxing. I mean half the world falls asleep with just the sound of the word meditation. Why were mine such a fucking trip?

I walked into the kitchen and started the coffee. I sat on the couch in a state of contemplation.

I began to pray.

"God, what the hell is going on?"

"Am I going crazy?"

One thing I've learned over the years is that if you're going to ask God something, you have to shut the fuck up after and wait for your answer.

So, I waited patiently.

Suddenly, I became aware of an angel in my kitchen. He was timeless.

"My name is Alfin," he said.

"All is well with you. Just go with it. Have fun. You are and have never been alone."

HOLY SH*T I'M A F***NG PSYCHIC

A deep sense of peace took over me and I lost track of time in my silence.

Ivana appeared into the living room.

"Babe are you ok?" she asked as I came to.

"Yes," I said.

"Yes, I am and have always been ok!"

A BRIEF LOOK INTO MY THOUGHTS IN FEELINGS

As I grew more confident in my psychic abilities, I felt the courage to begin to share my gift with more and more people. However, I was greeted with weird looks from some of my clients. I shared with others my stories, and they were in disbelief. Business colleagues stopped calling Ivana and I and work slowed down for her after she mentioned my "new gift".

So, I sought advice from a close acquaintance who has been a psychic medium for over twenty years. He completely dismissed me, and this broke my heart.

I struggled hard to comfort myself through prayer. My meditations and my psychic abilities could only be understood by those who have had similar occurrences.

I mean, it's not like I can call up someone and ask for advice about the freaking ancient bird that told me shit through his eyes during a meditation. Or that I knew that the guy that just walked by me with his sweet little family had a hidden prescription to a porn site. I couldn't sit in a group conversation and tell people how everything was covered in red velvet in one of my meditations or that the bartender's mom wanted her to move to a different apartment because her cat needed more sunlight. Imagine this, "What's new Veronica?" "Oh, I have a new friend, his name is Alfin, he's an angel." Give me a fucking break. If I shared that with anyone, I would be 51-50'd in two seconds!

Had I come so far from the crystal meth homeless weirdo only to become a "psychic weirdo"?

I felt so alone but grateful for the comfort and answers I found in my meditations. Soon, I realized that instead of seeking advice from others I would pave my own way. I would share my story so that the younger generations had a handbook of what happened to me. I wanted to share everything so that others didn't feel crazy or alone, like I felt. I wanted them to know, that I believed them. Honestly, at this point, I fucking believed everything!!

I decided to travel the world to speak about my psychic healing ability and ended up getting a speaking coach to teach me how to do it without using the word fuck.

SLOVAKIA 2022

RECAP:

No matter how hard we tried to continue to live in Long Beach, we just could not settle back in. Don't get me wrong, my practice is healthy and always growing and Ivana can work anywhere. But by now, we had begun to hate the smell of LA bullshit. Our condo was destroyed during a hellish never-ending remodel and so was our dream of having a beautiful home in Long Beach. Experiencing life in Slovakia, with family and genuine friends made us hypersensitive to what we lacked in California.

I always wanted to live in Europe, and I worked for over three years to convince Ivana to move. And with all the success she had last year, I felt strongly that our move had finally come. I began to convince Ivana that she was Slovakia's prodigal son returning to claim her inheritance. I convinced her that she was Slovakia's Sandra Bulluck/Slovakia's sweetheart. So, in May of 2022, we happily returned to Slovakia.

*On our last morning, during our gratitude walk, I found a second black feather. I picked it up without hesitation.

CASE NAME: ALARM CODE

We manifested a home in Devin. Yes, you read that right. In September of 2021, we met a man one time who eventually ended up allowing us to stay in his beautiful and magical villa. It had sat vacant for over two years just waiting for us. It is located in an area of Slovakia that was first settled in the stone age and

HOLY SH*T I'M A F***NG PSYCHIC

has magic up the Ying yang. The night skies here are insane and the sounds of nature sooth even the hardest of souls. Reindeer roam about freely in between cottages and modern homes. A castle sits a top of a hill overlooking the crossing of the Danube and Morava Rivers.

As mentioned in earlier chapters, we stayed in this home in January and February of 2022 prior to returning to California. I was able to finish my first book in the stillness of the town's peaceful days, and Ivana was able to get peaceful sleep in the town's quiet nights. The home enveloped us both in its loving energy and made us so happy. So, naturally when we returned, we asked if we could stay again. We were greeted with grace, and we gratefully moved back in.

Every time, we left for more than a day, we messaged our friend and owner of the house to let him know. He would then turn on the home's alarm remotely. Before our arrival, we sent him a text and he would disarm the alarm remotely. This system worked well for all of us.

On the first Sunday back, we were invited out of town to celebrate a birthday. Because of Slovakia's zero tolerance on alcohol while driving law, we planned to spend the night out of town just in case we wanted to drink.

By the evening our jetlagged kicked in so I decided not to drink, and Ivana didn't drink because they didn't have any champagne. We decided to leave back home which would put us back in town around midnight.

HOLY SH*T I'M A F***NG PSYCHIC

We sent out several WhatsApp messages announcing our arrival, but they were left unread, and we didn't get a response. When we arrived, we took a chance on entering the home anyway. We thought we would try and enter in case he had read the message and simply not responded.

As I opened the front door, the alarm went off. I literally felt like I was on an episode of COPS but proceeded to go inside any way. Ivana waited outside, of course.

Sure, let the Mexican go down for it, I thought.

The town itself is pitch black at night so you can imagine the darkness in the home. Despite the blaring alarm, I remained calm and centered. I'm blind in the dark so I worked through the entry and into the kitchen by feeling my way on the walls. I was afraid to turn on the lights just in case that would set off another round of alarms, so I worked my way in the darkness towards the sound of the alarm. I opened the door to the laundry room and found the alarm's keypad. Luckly I was tall enough to reach it. I flipped it open and entered a random generic code, like 123456. The alarm continued blaring in the stillness of the night.

A calmness took over me. I closed my eyes and placed my left hand over them. I placed my right hand over the keypad and allowed my fingers to move on their own. To my amazement I entered the correct code and the alarm shut off!

I turned on the light and motioned Ivana to come inside. We both stared at each other in disbelief.

"What the fuck did you do?" she asked.

HOLY SH*T I'M A F***NG PSYCHIC

I told her exactly what I had done.

"Fuck, Fuck, Fuck, Fuck, "Fuck, Fuck, Fuck, Fuck, "Fuck, Fuck, Fuck, Fuck, I said shaking my hand and brushing my fingers off on my clothes. I could still feel the energy and the plastic keypad on the tips of my fingers.

We waited for the alarm to go off again and for a million police officers to storm in and question us and haul me away, but the silence of the night took over.

We went to bed mind fucked again unable to talk about the incident.

Ivana and our friend, the owner of the house, texted back and forth and she told him what I had done.

She told him the code that I had entered.

"Well, you don't have to text me anymore," he said jokingly.

I could not believe it. How in the world did it do that?

How did I know the code?

*Quick question about this chapter, do you think I used too many fucks?

THE TALK: MAY 2022

"Babe, I think by now you know that you should be seeing clients for psychic sessions, don't you?" I looked at Ivana as she talked to me with her mouth full. (She loves eating the food I cook for her.)

"I am going to start telling people that you have this beautiful psychic gift." Would you like to start seeing clients for this?"

HOLY SH*T I'M A F***NG PSYCHIC

"Shit!" "What?" "No, please" thoughts raised through my mind as I stuffed avocado toast in my mouth to avoid answering her. To my surprise my head nodded yes.

"Yes!"

She smiled and said, "I will translate for you!"

I tried desperately to come up with excuses as to why I couldn't do it, but I truly felt like I could.

"Yes," I said "I will trust my gift."

After the whole alarm incident, I had begun to feel more settle into it and had stopped myself every time doubts flooded my brain.

"These are my conditions," I said hoping to regain some sort of control.

1- I don't want to know how much they will pay for my psychic healing sessions. I don't want to see any money.

2- I don't want to know anything about them prior to their psychic healing session. I do not control my schedule. I just want to know the day before how many people I will see so that I can prepare.

3- If I do not feel comfortable, I will stop the session. I will not be forced into anything that is not from God.

Ivana gladly agreed.

HOLY SH*T I'M A F***NG PSYCHIC

One day she posted my picture along with a brief description about my psychic gift on her Instagram stories. Her phone was instantly flooded with session requests.

I had no clue how to prepare for this. I prayed to God on my gratitude walk. I walked up to the Devin Castle every day. I walked through its dense green forests and fell in love with all the trees and sounds. I felt at peace in nature.

*I think at first, I felt secure because Ivana was by my side as an interpreter. Her presence kept me calm.

MEMORABLE CASES

All of the following sessions are translated by Ivana except for the ones with an *

CASE NAME: THE FLOWER

One day, I ventured on a different direction for my gratitude walk. There was a cold chill in the air, so I wore a heavy white sweatshirt. As I walked, I was overwhelmed by the number of bugs in the air. The walking trail ended, and I was forced to compete with cars on a narrow road. The energy in the air was mystical. I walked for quite some time before realizing that I would have to be on the street with cars for a very long time. So, I decided to turn back. When I turned around, a bright orange flower stood up in the middle of a field to the side of me. I walked over to it and pulled it out of the ground. I walked with it in my hand back home.

93

HOLY SH*T I'M A F***NG PSYCHIC

I felt like I was in a daze, really as if I was out of touch. My mind was foggy and empty. I focused on the flower to stay alert. The few cars that drove by passed right beside me, I felt out of place. But I had no other place to walk. I was trapped between a field, a road, and a rocky mountain.

At one point, I looked at my white sweatshirt and it was covered in bugs. I quickly brushed them off with my hands. I did this many times, each time the bugs grew in numbers.

That day, I had my first psychic healing session. The gal was grieving.

"Can you connect to her?" she asked as tears flooded her eyes.

I closed my eyes, and I could feel her friend's energy. I described her last days as she battled cancer. Her friend's energy told me to describe everything that I felt on my walk earlier that day. The feelings of loss and confusion. The feelings of emptiness and being trapped. So, I did. I described my walk, and it all took shape. I then took my hands and showed her the movements I made to remove the bugs that gathered on my sweatshirt.

"She shows me that she's covered in it," I said. "Her cancer spread."

"Yes," these are the motions she did in the end," she said.

The way the signs for my psychic healing session came to me where super vague but weirdly, I understood them, and she understood me. They all made sense to her. It was like I was playing a game of charades.

I heard her friend's voice inside me say, "Go get that flower you pulled earlier on your walk."

HOLY SH*T I'M A F***NG PSYCHIC

I ran inside and grabbed the flower.

"She said for you to paint this." I said as I handed her the orange flower.

"Yes, I just started to paint," my client said.

"When you finish the painting, she will visit you in a dream," I said.

"I've been asking her to visit me in my dreams," she said.

"I hope that she does."

After the psychic reading, Ivana asked, "how the fuck did you know all of that?"

I told her about my walk and how I felt a voice tell me to simply describe my walk and then answers just flowed out of my mouth.

My soul knew instantly to go for walks prior to any psychic healing sessions. So, I did.

CASE NAME: MESSAGE FROM GRANDPA

As I made my way down the hill towards Devin Castle, I asked God to send me an angel. I finished my walk and as I walked the long hill back to our house, I stopped to touch a beautiful purple flower and its leaves. I did this with everything. Rocks, trees, flowers. I was surrounded by nature, so I was like a kid in a candy store.

As I marveled at the flower, an old man walked up to me. He looked like he was made out of dirt. His teeth looked like stained sandstone and his nails looked like they belonged on a prehistoric animal. I could tell his age by the cloudiness around

95

the pupil of his eyes. His smile was warm, and his eyes were love. He looked like a real-life gnome.

He began speaking to me. I waited for him to stop so that I could tell him that I didn't understand him, but he didn't stop talking. He pulled the flower out and ate it, then continued talking to me. I finally was able to tell him that I did not understand him, but he didn't care. He talked and talked anyway. He pulled another flower out and ate it again. Then he pulled another one and offered me a bite. I said a quick prayer and took a big bite. It was bitter as fuck, so I quickly chewed.

He continued to talk and somehow, I began to somewhat understand what he was saying. I thought maybe the flower was hallucinogenic because I understood he was talking about something to do with blood and heart. At this point I didn't understand Slovak language one bit.

He then grabbed my wrist and walked me over to a metal sign sticking out from an empty dirt field. He licked his finger and dragged it on the dirty sign leaving a series of numbers on the sign.

I managed to make him understand that I did not understand him, and he finally gave up. He kissed my hands, and I kissed his and off he went. I knew it was an angel.

As soon as my next client came to see me, I knew her grandfather had a message for her. I described the old man and his love of herbs and flowers to her. "Yes, that's him, she said."

I then gave her a message of love and hope based on my interaction with the old man.

HOLY SH*T I'M A F***NG PSYCHIC

I began to understand that my messages would come from signs in my everyday life. I knew deep inside that I must be alert and ever present to see the signs.

*CASE NAME: MY GRANDDAUGHTER

I took my FBI clearance, passport, and some euros and ran out to meet my Uber driver. I looked forward to my ride because I love the drive from Devin into Bratislava. The narrow two-way road is adorned with large trees interrupted by little stacks of homes here and then trees again. The trees grow tall from each side and touch each other on the tops creating a tree tunnel. The road runs along the Danube River. I always connect to the trees and talk to them with my thoughts.

I got dropped off in the old town and walked with the direction of my navigation. I was enroute to get my documents translated to begin my visa process.

I had visited the office with Ivana before, so I was kind of familiar with whom I was supposed to communicate with. As I walked, I kept my eyes on the cobblestones to make sure I didn't trip. The ground in the old town can be a bit uneven. As I approached the office, I spotted a feather that told me to pick it up. I walked towards it, and I could smell vomit. I looked about a foot away and someone had puked their guts out.

I picked up the feather and said, "You little fucker, why did you make me pick you up here by the vomit?" I looked at it, it was white, gray, and black. It told me it represented disconnection of mind, body, and spirit.

97

HOLY SH*T I'M A F***NG PSYCHIC

I walked into the office and the old woman whom I expected to see was not there. Instead, a young lady was there.

"My grandmother is not here today but I will take care of you," she said.

After we finished our business and I gathered myself to leave she said,

"My grandmother wanted me to ask you if you knew anyone that is a healer."

I felt a huge smile form on my face, and I heard my mouth move and say, "I am a healer!"

"Yes, my grandmother thought so."

"Can we book an appointment with you?"

I gave her Ivana's information.

The very next day, Ivana tells me, "Babe you have a last-minute appointment today." "I am sorry, but this person is traveling from Belgium, it is kind of an emergency."

I prepared myself all day by staying in a calm space. That afternoon, I see the old lady that knew I was a healer walk into meet me with her ill granddaughter in tow.

The feather told me what she needed, and I was able to comfort her.

Near the end, when I had gathered her trust, I said, "You've struggled with anorexia and bulimia far too long." (I focused in on the puke that splattered next to the feather the day before.)

Her eyes grew big, and she nodded softly, yes.

"Today, I heal you from that too!" I said as I took her limp frail body into mine.

I touched her and loved her, and prayed for her, and cleansed her mind, body, and soul. Her session went on for over an hour. In the end, she left revived and happy. Her grandmother hugged me on her way out. She was not very affectionate by nature, but I knew she was proud of me, and she knew I was indeed a healer.

THE PREPARATION

"I only want to schedule morning psychic healing sessions from now on," I said as I walked into the kitchen one day. "I am feeling drained with just the simple preparation of it all."

Ivana took a zip from her coffee and said, "OK babe, I will schedule my tattoo clients later so that I can help you translate in the morning."

I began to develop this feeling of self-isolation and deep quietness took over me on the days that I knew I had a psychic healing session. I woke up and meditated to center myself. I did not interact with Ivana much and her simple touch and her voice sometimes disturbed my concentration. I did not drink coffee instead; I drank tea with local honey.

One day, as I reached for my toothbrush, I heard, "No, don't brush, not before your psychic healing sessions." So, I stopped brushing my teeth on those mornings. Pretty gross but true. I was filled with calm energy that also didn't allow me to eat. I just wanted to sit and hum before my client came to see me.

"Open and close in prayer," I heard one day as I zipped on my tea. "Don't forget to use sage and palo santo." So, from then on, I did.

CASE NAME: THE WALKS THAT TALK

One day as I walked to Devin castle. I heard a voice that said, "All bodies are recycled so pay close attention."

I walked over to the bank of a lake that forms when the Morava River overflows. I saw three kids playing together. The older sister must have been around ten years old, the younger sister about seven, and the little boy about three or four. Although, I do not understand Slovakian language, it was very evident that the older sister was verbally abusive to the younger siblings, especially to the little boy.

I watched as she continued to brutalize them and held back from saying anything only because she let off. I gave her a couple of dirty Mexican mom looks but they went unnoticed.

Their mom sat a few yards away from them and stared at them with a blank stare. She didn't react or seem to care. Their screams went unnoticed, and her blank stare wondered through them and unto the lake.

I looked back at the older little girl, and she looked at me with hate. I looked at her with love and it made her uncomfortable.

I stayed around long enough to ensure the little bitch wasn't going to kill her siblings. After a while, she gathered her brother and sister and walked them up to her mom.

HOLY SH*T I'M A F***NG PSYCHIC

"Mama, mama," they screamed trying to gain her attention. She just looked at them and nodded yes. I could tell she was either drunk, tired of them, or depressed. Then I thought, hell if I was that little bitch's mom, I would be drunk, tired, and depressed too.

I wanted to continue to focus on how I would feel if I had to deal with that awful kid when I was stopped in my thoughts.

I was immediately filled with love for the hateful little girl. I recognized her hate as the sadness I once experience myself as a child.

I whispered a prayer for them and wished them well.

The next day, I knew that the angry little girl was my client and her family.

"I am sorry for what you had to go through while growing up," I said as we started our psychic healing session.

"You were left alone to mother your sister and baby brother and that made you so mad."

"Yes," she said sadly.

I knew that she was heavy with guilt.

"Don't feel guilty anymore, today I will do a cleanse for you to raise you out of this guilt vibration."

"I was not very nice to my brother and sister," she said.

Before she could continue, I said, "especially to your little brother."

"I want you to know that your mom was not ok. Her marriage was not ok. Her life was not what she wished for. She suffered from alcoholism and mental illness."

"Yes, I know," she said.

A private message of love and hope followed.

"I want you to call your brother and apologize to him. He did not have the tools to deal with his childhood trauma."

"Your apology will not only liberate him, but it will heal you as well."

"I will call him today," she said.

After she left, of course Ivana was mindfucked.

"Babe, how the fuck did you know all of that?" Ivana asked me with excitement.

"I saw it on my walk to the castle," I said.

I described to her what I had experienced, and we were both blown away.

"How do you know who to look at and how do you decipher the message?" she asked.

"I listen to God," I said.

From then, I began to rely on my walks for answers to my psychic readings and they were 100% accurate. Always!

CASE NAME: GRANDPA'S MURSE

As I approached the lake, I looked around and saw a heavy-set old man sitting on a bench with what appeared to be his grandson. By the bench laid an old empty beer can. As I got closer, the "grandpa" got up and chased after his young grandson. He caught up to him and held him by the hand. They

102

walked joyfully together as he pointed things out to him. He talked to the toddler as they walked hand in hand. I noticed in the other hand he held on to a black murse. (Man Purse)

The image was burned into my brain.

The next day, as I prepared for my client, I knew that was her dad and her son.

"Your dad wants me to tell you that he is ok." "The way he drank eventually caught up to him and that is why his liver failed." "His diet wasn't going to help him either, but being heavy set runs in your DNA, so don't be ashamed of your weight."

"Yes," she said.

"He died with complications of the liver; he drank so much. I sure wish I could lose weight, but yes, we are all bigger people," she said smiling.

"Your father also wants you to know that he is always watching over your son. Every move he makes, he watches. He is literally holding him by the hand. Stop worrying so much about him. He will be just fine."

"She wiped her tears and said, "OK I will trust. I have been worried sick; he is always getting into something."

"But he is always right there with him showing him the way," I said.

"Tell him, if he listens close enough, he will hear his grandpa's voice and know his direction."

"Your father also wants me to tell you that he is protecting all of your finances and real estate investments."

"Oh, my," she said. "I have been so worried about my last real-estate investment. Should I sell it?"

"No, hold on to it, he is watching it. All your money is safe."

The rest of the psychic reading flowed out of me with sweet gentle ease.

CASE NAME: HIS BROTHER & UNCLE

I walked in sweet silence and looked up at the clouds. One cloud formation stood out because it glowed purple and green. As I continued along the Danube, I noticed two young boys sitting on a huge rock down by the river's edge. They were young, their bodies lean and healthy. They sat opposite each other enjoying a good laugh. I knew what I was seeing was for my psychic reading. I then breathed in a somber breath. I walked to a memorial and sat down on a bench. The memorial is engraved with about four hundred names of people who died when the iron wall fell. One name stood out from all the rest.

"Your brother wants to remind you of all the good laughs you had," I said to my client as soon as our psychic healing session began.

He was touched immediately.

"Yes, I was hoping that he would visit me today," he said.

"Who is Gustav?" I asked him.

"He is my uncle; I am staying at his house while I visit Slovakia. He has passed and my aunt lives alone."

"Give your auntie a kiss from Gustav, please.

"Your uncle and your brother are here with us now," I said.

104

HOLY SH*T I'M A F***NG PSYCHIC

"Your brother is showing me the color purple and green," I said. He nodded.

"He wants you to take a walk down to the Devin Castle. Walk along the Danube River. Stop by the memorial and talk to him there that is where he died," I said.

"Yes, he drowned. His body turned up later in the river in Bratislava."

"How did he die?" He asked me.

"He was killed many years ago where the two rivers meet. He was hanging with the wrong people."

"Yes, it's been many years, I was so young. They were never sure of how he died because his body was decomposed by the time it was recovered." He said sadly.

"He did not drown he was shot several times and thrown into the river. By time he hit the water, he was dead."

A message of love and hope continued. His brother and uncle's energy filled our space. In the end, we were filled with peace.

*I cannot explain how this happens. I do not know how I know specific details and names. In sessions like these, the words just come out of my mouth as though I have no control of what I am going to say. It is like the spirit that is using me to communicate with their family takes over and talks to them through me. I speak with such conviction that I am mesmerized and astonished in the end.

CASE NAME: EVERY LITTLE THING IS GONA BE ALRIGHT

I got out of bed on a beautiful summer morning feeling amazing after my meditation. I looked at myself in the mirror and sang myself a love song which I made up as I sang. I looked deep into my brown eyes and told myself that I loved every part of my body. (This is my daily routine; I do this without fail for at least two minutes every day.)

As I sang, I began to think about my speaking coach. I thought about what I should say to her to make her believe in me. I really wanted to impress her. Then, I released the thought because it was useless. (I tend to blog down my mind with useless shit sometimes, luckily now I catch myself.)

As I focused on creating another scenario in my head, the song "Everything's gonna be alright" came into my head and I hummed it while brushing my teeth.

After I was done, I tested the acoustics in the bathroom and sang it as loud as I could. I imagined I was on American's got talent impressing the shit out of the judges. But, before I got the golden buzzer, I hear Ivana yell,

"Babe, please! Please babe! My ears are bleeding!"

"I can not have these disturbances in the morning, please honey, stop!"

I smiled my evil grin in the mirror. Despite, what she may think, I know she loves my singing. So, I continued all the way up into the kitchen where she sat drinking her coffee.

106

HOLY SH*T I'M A F***NG PSYCHIC

I kissed her on the forehead and poured myself a cup of coffee. A few seconds later, she too was humming the song. I thought about my speaking coach and sang that song all day until that evening when I texted her the following:

Wednesday, June 15, 2022
Hi Dame Didi
Don't Worry about a thing, every little thing is gona be alright. Little birds singing sweet songs.

Thursday, June 16, 2022
She sends this pic:
And her text: Did you see what's on the top of the building?
The hotel where she had arrived in Zurich.
"EVERYTHING IS GOING TO BE ALRIGHT"
Pretty crazy hu? I don't know, some call its coincidence. I call it "holy shit"

CASE NAME: FRIEND CAN YOU HELP ME FIND MY WEDDING RING?

It was a warm Sunday afternoon, and my book sales were hot that week. We were in Kostolne, at Ivana's mom's house. She made us homemade dessert and coffee and we all sat outside in her garden. (Ivana gets a kick out of personally packaging everything that sells from her eshop.) I signed books, Ivana addressed them, and her mom sealed the envelope. In the middle of our "workshop" I got a text from our dear friend in Montecito California that read:

"July 13, 2022, 5:46 pm *Sweet friend! I need your help! I lost my wedding ring; I am so bummed! I have looked everywhere for it and can't find it. I think I might have thrown it away by accident at work, maybe slipped off while taking gloves off. We already went through the trash and could not find it. The weird thing is that it is also our 19th anniversary on the 5th. Do you think I will find it or is it gone?????*

I calmed her down with a few random texts because I knew that her wedding ring was not lost. Then, I instinctively knew to get up and go burry my face into the grass. (BTW I am completely freaked out by all the shit that roams in a garden, like bugs and spiders. But for some reason I didn't care.) I made my way into a corner of the garden and without hesitation, I kneeled and planted my face into the ground. I took a deep breath, then another, and then another. I could smell Mother Earth. A feeling of love arose from deep inside of me and I got emotional, but tears didn't flow. I loved Mother Earth.

After a couple of seconds, I pictured myself walking into her home and up the stairs. I walked into her bedroom and turned into her master bathroom. I looked to the left and saw a pile of towels. I could see through the towels and through the counter. I saw the ring in the towels.

HOLY SH*T I'M A F***NG PSYCHIC

At 5:51pm, I sent her this text: *Check in your restroom by towels*, then I gave her instructions on how to do it. Minutes later, she called.

"I found my ring in the towels! I found my ring! Veronica, I had been looking for it for three days! I was so scared that it was gone!"

Ivana, her mom, and I were mind blown. I gave God the glory and by now it was beginning to feel natural.

CASE STUDY: ACCIDENTAL HYPNOSIS

My dear friends asked if I could see them for one of my healing sessions. It was still a bit weird for me to do a psychic reading on my friends, but I agreed.

It is amazing to me how God, my angels, my guides, and the energy of those that have passed on all look out for me, send me signs, and use my voice.

I was directed to a meditation that I became addicted to. It is a centering exercise meant to relax the physical and mental state resulting in a healthier state of mind. The more I meditated the better and more in tune I felt during my psychic readings.

One day, our friend who is about eight feet tall and two hundred pounds arrived for his energy cleaning session. I knew exactly what to do.

I asked him to lay down and I repeated the meditation I had been practicing word by word. (I had it memorized by this point.)

In the end, he opened his eyes and said, "That is the first time in my life that I did not feel pain in my feet. Because of my size, I suffer from pain on my knees, back, and feet. I was completely relaxed and felt like I was floating."

Days later, I had a client of comparable size, I repeated the meditation on him. He too, floated into a state of deep relaxation. When he opened his eyes, he wept.

"I feel like I was hypnotized," he said.

After he left, Ivana looked at me with disbelief.

"Holy shit babe, I think I hypnotized these men!" I researched the meditation a bit more and realized that it was a deep relaxation or self-hypnosis therapy.

I continued to practice it myself three times a day and integrated it into my psychic healing sessions.

CASE NAME: CLAUSTROPHOBIA PART. 1

I got a call from Ivana one day. "Babe sorry for the last-minute call, but you have a client this afternoon, sorry but it's an emergency."

Hours later, I sat in front of a shy lady who sported a fresh tattoo on her arm. "I just tattooed her," Ivana said.

"I figured that much babe, even if I didn't have psychic abilities, I think I would know that," I said quietly under my breath.

I did not have any signs during my walk so I asked my client, "Why did you want to see me?"

"With your powers, you can't tell?" she asked.

"No, I am sorry," I answered her honestly.

110

"I suffer from claustrophobia."

As soon as she said that I knew when it started and how she would begin to heal.

"It started during your divorce," I said.

"Yes," she answered.

"I want you to go home and take a bath everyday for the next month."

"I haven't taken a bath in many years," she said.

"I can not fly on an airplane, so I haven't been able to travel."

I gave her instructions on how to turn her bath into a personal ceremony.

CASE NAME: DEAD BIRD

I held my green teacup close to my body and went outside. I hummed in preparation for my client. When I moved the couch to prepare our seating area, I saw a dead bird under it. As I wrapped it gently to dispose of it, I began to hear beautiful angelic sounds in my head, so I hummed along.

When my client came in, I instinctively knew the bird was her grandfather.

"Your grandfather is here," I said.

Her eyes filled with tears.

"He had a terrible deadly accident but wants you to know, that he is ok."

"His body was completely shattered but he did not suffer," I said.

"Honestly, he didn't even feel it."

"I loved him dearly, I wanted him to be here today," she said through her tears.

"He wants you to stop feeling guilty for not being able to see him in the hospital and wants you to know that he floated up with the angels and didn't feel his body."

"Please stop thinking about his injuries because when he died all he heard were beautiful angelic songs that comforted him."

"Yes, yes," she said.

"Ok, Ok, I will."

*Do not ask me about this case. This one was just unexplainable and super weird because I felt every answer from the dead bird.

A QUICK STOP TO TELL YOU ABOUT THE TREE

I forgot to tell you about this tree, I could go back and include the cases in the sequence that they happened in, but I've got a deadline to finish this book, so I'll make it quick.

In the beginning, I would look around everywhere for signs during my psychic readings, (which reminds me, I'll do more of this again) Anyway where was I?

Oh yeah, the tree. One day, as I prepared for my client, I looked at the tree in front of me. I talked to it and thanked it for being so glorious like me. I loved it and it loved me back. Weird shit but stick with me here.

"Look here," I heard the tree say in my head.

I looked down on its trunk at two protruding knobs.

112

HOLY SH*T I'M A F***NG PSYCHIC

"She has to check up on her breast surgery, remind her." I heard the tree say.

"Look down," I heard the tree again, so I did.

I looked at another protruding knob.

"She had issues with her belly button. You will need this information during her psychic healing session."

The session went as the tree advised.

About a month later, the tree did it again.

"Look at my bark." I did, it was red after the rain.

"Talk about his blood decease he had as a young adult."

"You will need this information during his psychic reading."

His grandfather came into the reading, and I was able to gain his trust by bringing up his blood decease to start the reading.

Weird shit hu?

CASE NAME: CANCER

My client walked in, and I could tell she was in a state of hopeless despair. I could feel her grief. I knew then that she had cancer. Later into our conversation, she said she feared death because she was ill.

"Yes, you have been diagnosed with cancer," I said as she began to cry.

"I have a doctor's appointment tomorrow and he will tell me if I must stay for surgery, I have cancer in my womb."

"You will be fine; you will not need surgery tomorrow." I said the words with so much power and faith that my entire body knew that through prayer I could heal her.

I laid her down to placed her into a deep meditation state. I placed my "illness" feather on her abdomen and led her into a complete physical and mental relaxation. Once she was completely relaxed, I prayed healing onto her entire body starting from her subatomic level.

After, I finished, we hugged, and she thanked me.

The next day, her husband contacted Ivana to tell her that my client did not need to stay for surgery. The doctor had released her, telling her they would closely monitor her condition.

CASE NAME: 82-YEAR-OLD SWEETHEART

Back Story:

For about a week I struggled to sleep and during the day I was agitated and irritable. Soon, my agitation turned into internal rage. I felt mentally disturbed. This is far from my character; I can sleep in the front row at a Metallica concert sitting by the loudspeakers and I am very calm and no longer an angry person.

One day, I took my gratitude walk and my spirit lifted with happiness as I walked towards an elderly couple. I slowed down so that I could take in all their story. I was overwhelmed with love for them. They both looked at me and smiled as they walked by me.

HOLY SH*T I'M A F***NG PSYCHIC

On my return from the castle, I ran into them again. This time they sat lovingly on a bench. I memorized them and loved them from afar.

The next day, my client walked in with her elderly mother.

I knew that the couple I had seen on my walk were the elderly woman's parents. I began giving her a message of love and hope about her problem child.

"Your father wants me to tell you not to worry about him anymore," I said.

Her older son also came into the psychic reading and reassured her that he was also watching out for him from above. He informed her that most of his explosive outbursts were caused by his alcoholism and unstable mental condition.

"You have been the best mom so please stop blaming yourself," he said through me.

"He will get over this mom, but he is on his own soul mission, you know he has always been so different, since he was a child, you know he has always had difficulties," he said again through me.

He then said, "My brother behaves this way because he suffers from insomnia, and this is how he feels inside." I then described every emotion I felt through out the week. I talked about my sleepless nights and the manic behavior I had experience that week.

She looked deep into my eyes, and I felt her grief. We hugged each other for quite some time. She cried on my shoulder, and

115

HOLY SH*T I'M A F***NG PSYCHIC

I repeatedly told her that I loved her. "I love you sister," I said into her ear.

I then, placed her into a deep state of meditation and when I finished, she opened her eyes but was paralyzed into place. I sat next to her and rubbed her arm while she cried and cried. I looked deep into her eyes, they were blue and faded around the pupils. She looked deep into my eyes and felt my sincere comfort and love.

"I feel so much better," she said.

She sat down and I said, "we don't have much time on this planet, you know that!"

"So go and live a happy life from now on do not give in to guilt thoughts or vibrations. Enjoy your life, go for walks, and dance, dance as best as you can," I said as I held on to her soft hand.

"Yes, I will. I will do it because I have a new boyfriend and he loves to dance," she said.

After our session, I fell asleep. Later in my meditation I heard, "why are you not aware of the signs we give you? We were giving you signs about his character. The emotions you felt this week had nothing to do with you."

Later that week her daughter texted Ivana to thank her. She was so happy that her mom was finally calm and was not looking for any more psychics or fortune tellers. She had been spending so much money going to many people looking for comfort. But after my psychic reading, she was finally at peace.

Two weeks later, she died in her sleep. I love her and I know that I brought her peace before her passing. I am sure that I will see her again in another lifetime. "My sister".

CASE NAME: CLAUSTROPHOBIA PART 2

About a month after I saw my client that suffered from claustrophobia, I asked Ivana to bring her back. I wanted to place her into a deep meditation and do a cleanse of her mind while she was in a deep relaxation state.

She agreed to come back because she was desperate. She was scheduled to travel by plane and was terrified her claustrophobia would prevent her from her trip.

When she arrived, I placed her into a deep state of relaxation which led her safely into hypnosis. I prayed over her spirit and instructed the claustrophobia to leave her body.

A week later, she sent me a message on Instagram thanking me. She was back from vacation and had traveled by plane with no need of alcohol or medication. She had not been on a plane for twelve years. The claustrophobia was gone, and she was finally free.

THE SIGNS HAVE CHANGED

As life got more and more hectic for us, I feared that I wouldn't be able to bring my clients messages of love and hope because I wasn't always able to go on my walks to Devin castle.

I wondered how I was going to know when I didn't have time to go for my walks or when I was traveling or whenever I had psychic healing sessions in other parts of the world.

CASE NAME: THE BLACK EAGLE

Back Story: For several days, I felt the energy of a grandpa that came to play in one of the outside terraces.

As I prepared for my client, I got the urge to walk down into the lowest part of our home. It is an outdoor kitchen, that we seldomly hang out in. For some reason, I stared at a sticker of a black eagle that is on the sliding glass door.

As I walked back up to our house, I heard the grandpa energy say, "Google the spiritual meaning of black eagle. Hurry, and write it down this is a message for your client."

I picked up my phone and before I turned it on, I prayed, "God, please lead me to the correct site and give me the message for my client.

We all know that whenever we ask Google anything you will get millions of responses, but I knew the exact response that was intended for my client.

I began to write, and my hand moved like it was moving on its own. Soon a message appeared on the page.

"Your grandfather was here with his friendly funny loving energy and wanted me to deliver this message to you," I said.

I read him the message on the paper.

He nodded yes, the entire time.

"Does this message make sense?" I asked him mostly to reassure myself that I had done the right thing.

"Yes, it makes all the sense," he said smiling from ear to ear.

CASE NAME: THE STREET SIGNS AND THE SLUG

I went for my daily walk and prayed that God would use me during my next psychic reading. Instantly I saw messages in the street signs. I got home and quickly wrote them down so that I did not forget.

The next day, I entered a peaceful state as I zipped on my green tea. I was pulled up from where I sat, so I got up to walk the patio. I came across a huge slug. I heard Spirit tell me to go look up the spiritual meaning of a slug, so I did.

Before I Google searched, I entered into prayer, again, I found the exact message for my client.

I joined the message from the street signs and the messages from the slug and delivered a message of love, hope, and motherhood. My client nodded yes, and her eyes grew wider and wider as I spoke.

When I was done, I asked her, "does this make sense to you?"

"Yes, absolutely, it does!" She answered me with a big smile and threw her arms around me.

I began to understand that messages would be coming from different directions from now on. I knew to be always on high alert because the signs were changing.

CASE NAME: THE CROW AND CHAMPAGNE GLASS

One day at around four in the morning, I was awakened by the loud gawking of a crow right outside my window. Devin is a village where you can hear a pin drop. I got up and looked out the window but did not see the crow. I closed the window and went back to bed. As soon as I laid back down, the crow began to gawk again non fucking stop. I couldn't get back to sleep. So, I laid in bed and meditated.

"Did you hear that obnoxious crow?" I asked Ivana as soon as she woke up.

"No," babe I didn't.

Ivana's mom spent the night, so I asked her as well.

"No," she replied. She wakes up at the crack of dawn, so I didn't understand how she didn't hear it. How was it possible no one heard it? It was insanely loud!

I knew instantly that was my sign.

I walked into the kitchen and cleaned up a bit before my client arrived. There were a couple of champagne glasses on the counter. As I reached to put them away, I broke one. I was shocked because, I never break a dish. Ever! I knew from within to combine the crow and the broken glass signs and bring a message of love and hope to my client.

120

HOLY SH*T I'M A F***NG PSYCHIC

I knew instantly that my client's spirit animal, the crow was bringing in a message for her. I prayed prior to my Google research and within 20 minutes, I had a beautiful message for my client.

CASE STUDY: ME

Of course, I have doubts at times when I think about all that has happened to me in the past year. Especially if I listen to the haters on social media. One of the videos I posted got over five hundred thousand views and I asked Ivana if there were any negative comments. Ivana shared with me that someone wrote that I am not a psychic healer, that I am a drug addict who stayed high and is imagining all this shit and that I am taking advantage of people.

That comment didn't bother me because, I have been clean for almost ten years, but it did make me wonder. I wouldn't be human if I didn't wonder. I asked myself if this Googling spiritual meanings was right or what the fuck was it? I don't have a spiritual guide on how my gift works or what new signs I will get or what direction I will go. I do have prayer and my faith in God. So, I continue to trust that I am helping, and I am healing and that my psychic abilities are from God and are blessed by my ascended masters, guides, and angels.

One day, as I prepared for my client, I had another animal sign. But I chose to ignore it and continue with my quiet meditation. In the stillness I heard God's voice say, "What the hell?" Don't you dare ignore this sign, get your little ass in there and research what that means and compose a message of love and hope for your client." I jumped up from the couch and did exactly that. That day, I chose not to doubt my psychic journey.

*I am on this journey that has changed my life radically. I know that if I listen to God and have clean intentions, I will be used as a liaison between humans and the spiritual realm. Honestly, I don't know where this will lead but I am game for any of this weird shit in my life. So, I will listen to God and be aware of signs no matter how they come or where they come from.

CASE STUDY: THE PHONE SPEAKS

One day as I prepared myself to write all day, I got a WhatsApp message from my friend asking if she could come over and simply hang out. Typically, I immediately say no to these types of requests. I have a tough time hanging out, I must do something productive with my day. (Unless hanging out means on a yacht in Saint Tropez) I knew instantly to answer yes.

Before I replied, I thought about how the night before, I had been bothered by a disruptive energy right outside my window. I knew it had to do with her. I don't know how to explain it. I just knew it. I knew I would have her over and I would tell her and pray over her.

As we laid out by the pool, I felt comfortable enough to tell her without scaring her. I try my best not to scare people or talk about negative shit in my psychic healing sessions. I only bring

122

messages of love and hope. I told her in a way that she would not find it scary. As soon as I brought it up, my phone began to play a song on its own. Mind you, my phone was under a towel, under my lawn chair. You have to enter a code to unlock it and you have to open the Instagram app and find the video for that song. We both instantly knew to pray over her before she left. So, we did. I believe prayer solves all and heals all. The bothersome energy didn't come back.

The next day, I walked through my favorite grocery store trying to talk Slovakian to all my friends there. As I walked through the aisles, I began to hear Spanish praise music. "Holy shit, that's cool," I thought. I couldn't believe that in a tiny village in Slovakia they were playing a Mexican praise song. And to make it even better, I knew it. I hummed along as I continued to shop when suddenly, I noticed the music was coming out of my grocery bag that hung on my shoulder. I reached in and took out my phone. The music was coming out of my phone. I entered my password and unlocked my phone as Pandora was blasting through out the store. I quickly turned it off because I did not want to look like a fool. When, I walked out of the store, I tapped on the app so that I could listen to the song on my walk home, but the app said "Pandora is not available in this country"

Things like these really touch me and remind me that there is so much that goes on around us that we do not get to see. These two instances with my phone reminded me to keep believing in the bizarre shit, keep trusting in God, and in my weird journey.

MY FEATHERS AND THEIR MEANING

1. FIRST FEATHER REPRESENTS: PSYCHIC ABILITY

   SHORT STORY: NUKU HIVA - One day, while we explored the jungle in Nuku Hiva, our guide stopped the truck to pick a local flower and give us a taste of ripened guava. Mexico memories flooded my brain as I bit into the guava, and I closed my eyes to take it all in. When I opened my eyes, I saw a black feather. I took it home with me to California. Later, I knew it represented psychic ability.

2. SECOND FEATHER REPRESENTS:
   SEEKING DIRECTION / HOME

   SHORT STORY: On our last morning, during our gratitude walk in Long Beach, California, I found a second black feather. I picked it up without hesitation, I knew it represented seeking direction about home.

3. THIRD FEATHER REPRESENTS: ILLNESS

   SHORT STORY: We joined our friends in Prague to celebrate a birthday. We met her close friends for the first time. When we sat down for dinner, I glanced over at one of them, and I instantly felt chest pain. I felt extreme exhaustion. As the dinner came to an end, he announced that he would be going home because he did not feel well. The couple left the table. A strong urge forced me to go join them outside. Even though I had just met him, I put my arms around him and held on to him. I prayed for healing. I held him close and took away his illness. I held him close and loved him. When I looked down, I saw a feather under my shoe. I waited until they got into the Uber. I picked it up and knew it represented illness.

4. FOURTH FEATHER REPRESENTS:
    DISCONNECTION / SPIRITUAL, MENTAL AND PHYSICAL
    SHORT STORY: In a walk-through old town, I looked down on the floor and picked up a feather. I looked at it, it was black at the tip, white in the center, and gray on the bottom. I picked it up and knew it represented disconnection of mind, body, and spirit.

5. FIFTH FEATHER REPRESENTS: ANGER
    SHORT STORY: We were invited to an event in Ostrava. I wore a sexy dress and high heels. Heels in Europe should be referred to as hells because they are impossible to walk in. I should have known better, but I wanted to look hot. We called Uber and happily made Insta reels on our way there. The Uber driver ended up dropping us off at the wrong venue. As soon as we walked out of the Uber, he sped off leaving us stranded in an abandoned arena. I looked around for a street but

125

all I saw was a huge empty parking lot which means fucked up heels and twisted and painful bunion feet. My anger began to boil up. Suddenly, it starts to pour rain! I was furious. We had to run to ensure we weren't completely destroyed. By the time we found cover I was fuming. I blew up on Ivana. Long story short, as soon as we walked into the VIP area at the correct venue, as the lady places the stupid paper wristbands, they make you wear at these events, I see a feather on the ground. I knew instantly, it stood for the absurd anger I had just let control my mood for over an hour. (It is very rare for me to be mad much less stay mad) I picked it up and knew it represented anger.

6. SIXTH FEATHER REPRESENTS: GRIEF

SHORT STORY: One day, I walked along the Danube River and the thought of my friend's aunt passing entered my mind. I wondered how she was dealing with her grief. I walked over to the edge of the river and said a quick prayer for her. When I opened my eyes, I was stepping on a feather. I picked it up and knew it represented grief.

7. SEVENTH FEATHER REPRESENTS: HOLE IN THE HEART

SHORT STORY: We invited Ivana's mom to stay with us to grieve the loss of her beloved friend of forty-one years. We went for a walk to help her clear her head. As we wrapped up our walk. I asked her, "how do you feel?" She smiled and held back her tears. I touched her back and she quickly said, "I have a hole in my heart." I looked down and there was a white feather with a black dot on it. I picked it up and knew it represented loss and suppressed emotions.

8. EIGHT FEATHER REPRESENTS: NIGHT TERRORS

SHORT STORY: I applied for a European Visa so that I could remain in Slovakia a bit longer. I was "forced" to remain in the European Union until my visa was approved. However, the visa took forever so Ivana and her mom ditched me and traveled to Seychelles for a week. I stayed home to focus on writing my two unfinished books. The first night I experienced severe night terrors. I was devastated because here I am "the healer" still dealing with bullshit trauma from my past. I went on a walk and prayed to God. I was so pissed off. During my walk God delivered me from guilt and blessed me with a beautiful message. On my way back home, I walked into the woods and found a feather. I picked it up and knew it represented night terrors.

I started taking my feathers into my psychic healing sessions every time. I don't have a clue as to why I felt the need to do so but I did. I began laying them out and asking my ascended masters for help.

127

CASE NAME: THE FEATHERS MOVED

One day, before my psychic healing session I laid my feathers out and said, "Feathers please move. Which ever one of you feathers moves, I will know that is a sign for my client."

I could feel faith oozing out of me literally. I visualized the feathers moving and I had my answer. Suddenly, two of the feathers moved. I almost shit myself.

It was the psychic feather and the sick feather.

When my client came in, I knew she was expecting a psychic reading and was dealing with illness.

"Why are you afraid of getting cancer?" I asked her right after our opening prayer.

Her eyes grew wide and filled with tears.

"My mom has cancer, and I am taking care of her."

"I think that I will get cancer too," she said looking at me scared shitless.

The session grew into a healing of the mind therapy. I don't remember much of the actual session, but I remember the freaking feathers moving! (Some of my sessions I forget instantly after I am done with the reading)

From then on, I asked my feathers to move, and they did. Sometimes, it will be a light breeze out of nowhere that will move them and other times, I blow softly over them. It is always the right feather for that psychic healing session.

Sometimes, I won't ask them for answers, I just use them to fan my sage and palo santo into my cleansing prayer.

ISOLATION AND SHADOW WORK

Ivana and her mom traveled to Seychelles, and I was forced to stay home alone. Something inside of me told me to enter a week of isolation. I decided to do a social media, food, and spiritual cleanse.

The first day was horrible. I experienced night terrors and the crippling fear that used to debilitate me as a child. I thought that I had overcome these fears but no matter how hard I prayed I couldn't get out of the debilitating terror state.

As I prepared myself to go to bed, my heart started racing fast and I panicked. I locked myself in the bedroom and froze in fear. I laid motionless watching the light from under the door looking for footsteps to come and find me. I then glanced at the window, knowing that the evil spirits would come in and haunt me. I prayed, held on to my feathers, and tried to place myself into self-hypnosis, but nothing worked. I finally passed out in the early morning. I felt defeated.

I struggled to understand why I was experiencing these terrible fears and emotions, after all, I was now a psychic healer! My first book detailed the horrors I experience as a child and even as I wrote about them, I didn't struggle.

I searched for God on my walk. "What the fuck God! What happened last night? How could you leave me like that! I thought I was healed!"

Before I finished with my demand for answers, I heard, "Healers can't be broken! Fix yourself! You have the tools; you even give them to your clients! Use them on you!"

HOLY SH*T I'M A F***NG PSYCHIC

I came home after my walk and Googled heart attack symptoms because quite honestly, I almost had one the night before!

About five minutes into the search and two seconds before I drove my dead body to the hospital from all the shit WebMD told me I would die of. I was led to "shadow work". I heard the term before but never knew what it was. I thought it was some weird witchcraft shit, so I never really cared about it. I knew exactly what I would do that evening.

That evening, when the fear creeped in, I grabbed little Veronica's hand and helped her heal her past traumas. My shadow work session took about an hour. After that I was completely calm. I did it for three days until my fear was completely gone. I realized that I had never healed from my night terrors and severer trauma I had endured as a child. After a week in isolation, I was ready to heal the world.

EPILOGUE / CONCLUSION

I was invited to speak at a convention in front of medical professionals and scientists and was encouraged to speak about how it feels to be the "new me" the psychic me.

So, happily, I submitted my talk title, "Holy Shit, I'm a fucking psychic". I waited patiently to see how it was going to be received. I got a quick response that read:

"Veronica, can we have a title that is more professional?"

I was instantly flooded with doubts. I played scenarios in my mind of how people were going to handle me and how negatively the world would receive my book.

"They will think that I am crazy, disrespectful, and a fool. For sure, they will shame me and publicly humiliate me." I thought to myself. What the fuck am I doing? I thought about withdrawing from the convention and changing the title of my book and my speech.

As I struggled to stand true to who I am and the reason why I chose to write this book, I ran across one of Ram Dass's audio recordings in which he described a woman that kind of reminded me of myself.

Ram Dass describes her something like this:

She had incredibly long false eyelashes and heavy mascara and a low-cut dress. She looked like something between Sophia Loren and Ana Magnani. She was foul mouth, uneducated, and didn't give a fuck.

131

HOLY SH*T I'M A F***NG PSYCHIC

Yet, she was used by God as a medium between Ram Dass and his guru Maharagi. When in the Samadhi State she taught Ram Dass Kabbala, geometry, mystic poetry, and spoke many languages among other things, I'm sure.

Hearing this recording made me realize even more that I don't have to fit into any mold or look like and act like Mother Teresa (who I love and respect). I don't have to change the way I talk or dress or even stop chewing my gum. Because God wants to use me just the way I am.

So, in conclusion, I think that my God has a good fucking sense of humor, and I am a very kind generous person who banked a shit ton of grace. I may be crazy, but we will never know until we die. So, in the meantime and while I am still alive, I will continue to know that "Holy Shit, I am a fucking psychic.

HOLY SH*T I'M A F***NG PSYCHIC

BIBLIOGRAPHY

1. MY LIFE MY STORY: "God, You Owe Me" by Veronica Belakova | Goodreads

2. https://youtu.be/fD_cijEkJXM

ACKNOWLEDGEMENTS

I would like to thank my angels, my guides, my ancestors who are all clapping for me because even though this is some weird shit, I am still going with it.

THE PEOPLE IN THIS BOOK: I would like to thank all the people in this book that trusted my psychic and healing messages.

SLOVAKIA: Thank you Slovakia, for making my first book top seller in your country. Thank you to all my sweet clients that have trusted me and Ivana (translator) with your psychic healing sessions. Thank you to Vlado and Lucia for allowing us in your villa where I can make my books come to life. Thank you to my family and friends in Slovakia for cheering me on.

PERMANENT COSMETIC CLIENTS: Thank you for waiting for me even though I will never tattoo again. Just kidding, thank you for your patience with me and my schedule.

ABOUT THE AUTHOR

Veronica's Career stops include Legislative Assistant for Long Beach Mayor Beverly O'Neill; Legislative Analyst for Councilwoman Laura Richardson; Community Engagement Director for the American University of Health Sciences; owner and operator of two restaurants and bars, and an event coordinator for a private financial planning firm.

Veronica graduated from Huntington Academy of Permanent Cosmetics in 2015 and opened the first Permanent Cosmetics Studio in Long Beach California.

Veronica's self-edited and self-published first book "My Life My Story, God, You Owe Me" landed on Amazon's New Hot Releases and became a best seller in Slovakia.

Veronica lives with her partner, Ivana Belakova. Together they travel the world removing stigmas and breaking barriers with their positive lifestyle seminars and "just Love" message.

To this day, Veronica has used her psychic healing abilities to help close to five hundred people and she does not plan to stop.

Currently Veronica spends her time between Montecito, California, Miami, Florida, Slovakia, and Dubai.

Made in the USA
Las Vegas, NV
15 November 2022

59528596R00074